The LEAPING SLIDING Sprinting RIDING Science Book

The Leaping Sliding Sprinting Riding Science Book

50 Super Sports Science Activities

Bobby Mercer

Illustrated by
Tom LaBaff

LARK BOOKS

A Division of Sterling Publishing Co., Inc.
New York

Editor
Veronika Alice Gunter

Art Director & Cover Designer
Robin Gregory

Creative Director
Celia Naranjo

Illustrator
Tom LaBaff

Copyeditor
Ron Wagner

Art Production Assistant
Bradley Norris

Editorial Assistance
Delores Gosnell,
Rose McLarney

Library of Congress Cataloging-in-Publication Data

Mercer, Bobby, 1961-
The leaping, sliding, sprinting, riding science book : 50 super sports science activities / by Bobby Mercer ; illustrated by Tom LaBaff. -- 1st ed.
p. cm.
Includes index.
ISBN 1-57990-785-7 (hardcover)
1. Sports sciences--Juvenile literature. 2. Sports--Experiments--Juvenile literature. I. Title.
GV558.M47 2006
796--dc22
2006020562

10 9 8 7 6 5 4 3 2 1

First Edition

Published by Lark Books, A Division of
Sterling Publishing Co., Inc.
387 Park Avenue South, New York, N.Y. 10016

Distributed in Canada by Sterling Publishing,
c/o Canadian Manda Group, 165 Dufferin Street
Toronto, Ontario, Canada M6K 3H6

Distributed in the United Kingdom by GMC Distribution Services,
Castle Place, 166 High Street, Lewes, East Sussex, England BN7 1XU

Distributed in Australia by Capricorn Link (Australia) Pty Ltd.,
P.O. Box 704, Windsor, NSW 2756 Australia

Every effort has been made to ensure that all the information in this book is accurate. However, due to differing conditions, tools, and individual skills, the publisher cannot be responsible for any injuries, losses, and other damages that may result from the use of the information in this book.

If you have questions or comments about this book, please contact:
Lark Books, 67 Broadway, Asheville, NC 28801
(828) 253-0467

Manufactured in China

ISBN 13: 978-1-60059-120-4
ISBN 10: 1-60059-120-5

For information about custom editions, special sales, premium and corporate purchases, please contact Sterling Special Sales Department at 800-805-5489 or specialsales@sterlingpub.com.

To Michele—I'm glad
we're a team.

Contents

The Most Fun You'll Ever Have with Science

Have you ever wondered what it is that spitballs do—besides sounding gross—that make them illegal in baseball? Do you want to know how to slam-dunk a basketball, or ollie on a skateboard? Are you ready to test your theory that it's just not possible for people to do the athletic feats you've seen on television—from back flips off a diving board to running nonstop for hours?

You've opened the right book. It's full of experiments for curious kids who like fun activities that get you moving, playing, and thinking. These 50 activities ask you to jump, bounce, run, slide, ride, roll, and more. You'll try them indoors, in your yard, on your driveway, at parks, and on sports fields. Because they're based on dozens of different sports, by the end you'll have tried everything from mountain biking and disc golf to tennis and basketball.

Thanks to the explanations, you learn the physics, biomechanics, and other science behind sports moves. Don't worry about how much science you already know. Putting on your thinking cap takes no more effort than putting on a baseball cap.

And you don't have to be on a team or train like an Olympic athlete to have fun playing a sport—or to use this book. A sport is anything active you do to have fun or get

exercise, from a simple game of catch with a friend to running with your dog to the park. An athlete is anyone who gets moving in order to have fun and feel good. So you have what it takes to do all of the activities in this book and try any sport you like.

You can do most of these activities alone, but it's fun to invite a friend or two to join you. On these pages you'll see Lucinda, Tim, Jessie, and Bobby demonstrating what to do.

Because he's a sports reporter for the school newspaper, Bobby always seems to have a notebook and pencil with him. They're handy for activities that ask you to record data you collect during your experiments.

Before you begin, read the How to Use this Book section on the next few pages. Then you'll be ready to test the theory that sports are the most fun you'll ever have with science.

How to Use This Book

The activities in this book let you test the how and why behind cool and quirky moves in dozens of sports. The explanations come from science—**chemistry**, **physics**, **aerodynamics**, **biomechanics**, and more. So you'll be stretching your muscles and your brain.

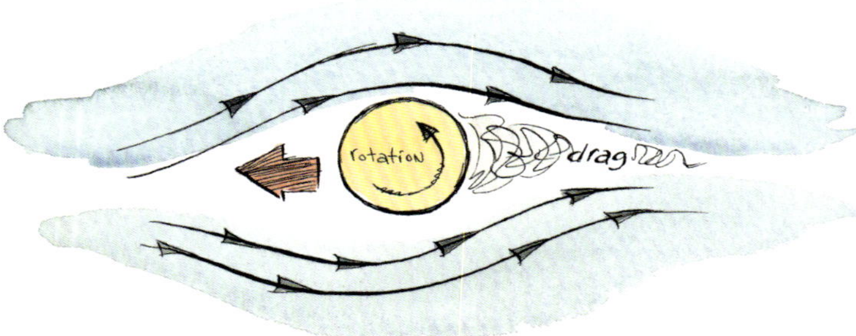

The Activities

Each activity includes a list of What You Need and instructions for What You Do. Read both sections before you start, so that you know exactly what you'll be doing, where, and with what. Gather your materials before you get started. It's easier and more fun if you're really ready before you begin an activity.

Sometimes you'll use sports equipment from around your house, such as different kinds of balls, racquets, bats, and your own bicycle. Other times you'll use equipment that has nothing to do with a particular sport. For instance, there's a water hose for All About Angles on page 32, your sneakers and a freezer for Get a Grip on page 18, and a flight of stairs for Watts Going On? on page 34.

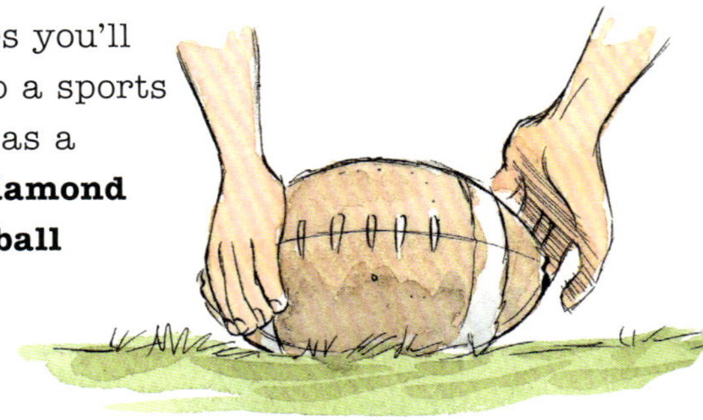

A few times you'll head out to a sports field, such as a **baseball diamond** and a **football field** for Baseruns on page 16. Observe the posted rules at any public or private sports field you wish to use.

After you try the activity, read What's Going On? to learn the science behind the sport. If you don't know the scientific meaning of the word **momentum**, or all about **Newton's laws of motion**, DON'T WORRY. You also don't have to be a walking dictionary of sports terms. You can find science and sports terms in bold (like **this**) in the glossary on pages 76 through 79. Tips and facts about different sports and more in-depth information about science are scattered throughout the book.

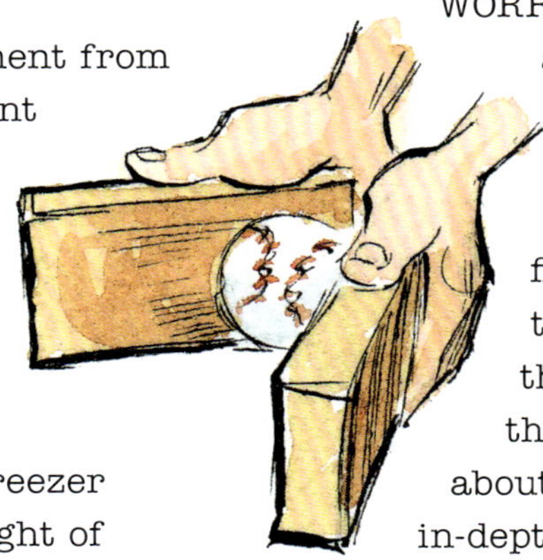

Stretch Your Brain

Every activity reveals something you probably didn't know about a sport. Find out how racecar drivers and cyclists put aerodynamics on their team so they can ride the air stream created by the car or bicycle just ahead. You don't need a racetrack—a candle will do. (See page 68.) Test why swimmers shave their hair—without getting into your swimsuit or pulling out a razor. (See page 19.) Have you ever wondered why a curveball "breaks" and a knuckleball "dances"? Why tennis players grunt? Why cyclists tuck into such a funny looking shape when they are going downhill? It's all in this book!

Stretch Your Body

You can take what you learn from these activities and use it on a court or playing field. For instance, turn to How Low Can You Go on page 38 to discover how to take down the competition in a **wrestling** match. You can learn the basics to throwing a **football**, and then become a better **quarterback** based on what you learn about **axes** and **velocity** in Spiraling Into Control on page 30.

Much of the science that explains each activity holds true across a variety of types of sport. So you can use your newfound science know-how to have more fun with any sport you play.

Most of these activities require just enough moving around to make you feel like you actually DID something with your body. But if you have any health problems, ask your parents to help you choose activities that would be best for you.

An Ollie By Golly

Use your feet to balance, spin, and push to make a board hop.

What You Need

- Flat, paved surface
- 3-foot long piece of lumber measuring at least 6 inches across and 1 inch thick
- Broomstick
- Skateboard
- Helmet
- Elbow and knee pads

What You Do

1. Place the broomstick on the flat, paved surface. Place the board (lumber) atop the broomstick lengthwise, with the broomstick in the center.

2. Stand on the lumber and try to balance over the broomstick so that neither end of the board touches the ground. (See illustration on page 13.)

3. Once you've mastered step 2, crouch down while balancing. Push down with one

foot and lift up the other without taking it off the board. The board should rotate around the broomstick as one end of the board hits the ground and the other end points up. If you can't do it right away, don't worry—it's a tough trick. Keep practicing.

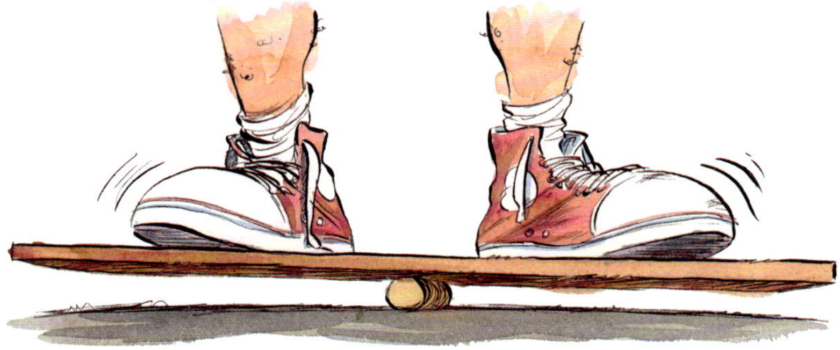

4. When you get your rotation down (step 3), it's time to take the move to the next level. Crouch down like before, but this time instead of pushing down gently, slam one end of the board down as hard as you can with your foot. If you do it right, you and the board will fly up off the ground.

5. Once you can make the board rotate (step 3) and hop (step 4), try it with the skateboard—without the broomstick. Make sure you're wearing your helmet and elbow and knee pads. Slam the end of the board to the ground and ride the front into the air.

What's Going On?

The **ollie** is a **skateboard** move for hopping over objects. It's a hard trick, so don't feel bad if you struggle with it. Some skateboarders spend months learning how to do it, and some never learn it.

The science behind an ollie is about shifting your weight and obeying **Newton's third law of motion** ("for every action there is an equal and opposite reaction"). Let's start with shifting your weight: when you crouch, you have a lower **center of gravity**. That makes it easier to keep your balance. Simple, huh?

Then you slam an end of the board into the floor. The **force** you exerted (to push down) makes the board **rebound** (push back up) off the floor. This rebound lifts the whole board—and you! That's because, following Newton's law, the floor supplies an opposite (upward) force equal to your (downward) slam. How fast you hop up depends on your **momentum** (the combination of your **speed** and **mass**). Try this experiment at different **momenta**. What makes for a good ollie?

Did your feet slide around on the piece of lumber? That should happen less on a skateboard. Skateboards have grip tape on their topsides, which provide the **friction** needed to hold your feet in place. Read more about friction in other activities in this book.

American Alan "Ollie" Gelfand is credited with inventing the ollie in 1976. He had only been skateboarding for two years!

Go For a Spin

Spin Bounces

Use friction to give a ball a spin and gain the advantage in basketball or tennis.

What You Need

- Basketball, soccer ball, or volleyball
- Smooth surface (try a wood or linoleum floor)

What You Do

1. Using one or both hands, give the ball a spin to the right as you let it fall straight down to the smooth surface. Which way did it bounce?

2. Now spin the ball in the opposite direction and drop it again. Which way did it bounce this time? Try spinning it toward your face as you drop it. Did it bounce back to you?

What's Going On?

When you spun the ball to the left, it should have bounced left. When you spun the ball to the right, it should have bounced right. With practice, you can throw passes that bounce around people. **Basketball** players use this spin trick to outwit **defenders**. You can, too, by using **friction** and **force**.

Friction is created when two objects make contact and one or both keep moving. Friction creates **resistance**, slowing the object down and/or causing it to change direction. In this activity, your challenge is to control the direction of the ball's bounce once it makes contact with the floor.

So, when you put the spin on the ball, you exert a bit of power, which requires **energy**. It's just enough energy to put some force (the demonstration of energy) into the ball's movement. When the ball hits the floor, that spinning force **rebounds** (is pushed back) in the direction of the spin.

Topspin

What You Need

- Tennis ball
- 2 tennis racquets
- Tennis court, or paved outdoor area or gym
- Friend

What You Do

1. Hit the tennis ball back and forth with your friend. It doesn't matter if you have a tennis net, set boundaries, or if you let the ball bounce before you hit it. Just get comfortable and get in a good rhythm.

2. Now that you are warmed up, try spinning the ball as you hit it. To do this, lift your swinging arm back in an arc so you drop the head (top) of the racquet down toward the ground. (Position your feet wherever it feels right.) When the ball comes into range, swing up and across your body so that when you hit the ball the racquet is about the height of your opposite shoulder. Practice this several times. You'll know you've hit a topspin when you see that the ball goes up into the air as expected but drops faster than your earlier hits.

3. Try making the ball spin to the right or left. What works—choosing a certain area of the strings to hit the ball with, twisting your wrist as you finish the hit, or something else? Finally, try to put backspin on the ball by hitting it from above. How is a backspin hit different from a topspin hit?

What's Going On?

A **tennis** player can make life tough on his **opponents** with **topspin forehands**, side-spinning **serves**, and **backspin lobs**. That's because anytime you put spin on a ball it moves in unexpected ways.

Controlling the ball's spin requires that you control the **friction** created when the tennis ball strikes your racquet. How do you do this? Smack the ball with just the right combination of **force** and racquet **angle**. The force powers the shot, the angle directs the shot. (You probably needed to practice several times to get it right. Tennis champs like **Venus Williams** practice a lot, too!)

Topspin lets you hit a tennis ball high enough to clear the net, but then the ball drops a lot sooner than your opponent might think. A **sidespin** makes the ball to go to the right or left. Backspins require that you push the ball down while quickly rolling it on the racquet back toward you. Can you hit a backspin?

Baserunss

Is the fastest route around a baseball diamond also the longest?

What you need

- Baseball field
- Football field
- Stopwatch or watch with second hand
- Friend
- Paper and pencil

What You Do

1. Head over to the closest baseball field with a friend or two, but remember that all fields aren't created equal. Youth-league fields have 60-foot base paths, which is the same as 20 yards. So a trip all the way around the bases is 80 yards, or 20 yards shorter than a football field. Adult fields, on the other hand, have 90-foot (30-yard) bases, with a trip of 120 yards from home to home.

2. Now it's time to run around the bases as fast as you can. Have your friend stand at home plate with the stopwatch and time you from start to finish. Switch places and time him. What were your times? Repeat this step to see if you can improve your time.

3. Make your way to a football field and figure out how far you need to run to match the distance you covered on the baseball field. If it was a youth field, get on one goal line and have your friend stand on the opposite 20 yard line, and if it was an adult field stand at the back end-zone line on one end with your friend all the way at the other back end-zone line. (End zones are 10 yards long, so the two of them combined with the regular field will equal 120 yards).

4. When you're ready, run the same distance you ran on the baseball field while your friend times you. How did it compare? Switch places and let your friend have a shot.

What's Going On?

You were a lot slower on the baseball field, weren't you? How come? Well, the biggest reason is because you actually ran a lot farther—probably farther than you thought you did.

Geometry has proven that the shortest distance between two **points** is a straight **line**. But bases aren't in a straight line. When you look at them from above, you can see that they form a diamond. To get around them efficiently, you must run a tight circle that ends up being a good deal longer than the actual straight-line distance between first and second, second and third, and third and home.

Why run the circle? Because it's faster than running straight and making a nearly complete stop at each base so you can turn left and head to the next one. Want more proof? Try it again—running from base to base in absolutely straight lines—and see how fast/slow you go.

Get a Grip

Can a freezer turn your sneakers into slippers? Find out with an on-your-feet traction experiment.

What You Need

- Sneakers
- Smooth wood or tile floor
- Large plastic bag
- Twist tie
- Freezer

What You Do

1. Put your sneakers on and practice some of your favorite sports moves on a smooth floor. You know, cut like you're playing defense against **LeBron James** or pretend you're dribbling around **Mia Hamm**. Your feet don't slide, do they? Of course not. That's why you wear sneakers to begin with.

2. Now take off your sneakers and place them in a large plastic bag. Press out all the extra air and tie the bag off with a twist tie.

3. Place the bag in the freezer and seal the bag well. Leave the sneakers in there for several hours.

4. Take the sneakers out and immediately put them on your feet. (If you have socks on you should be able to stand the cold.) Now carefully try those same sports moves on the floor. Can you feel the difference?

What's Going On?

You did a little unintended slipping and sliding in the cold shoes, right? People wear sneakers to play **indoor sports** because sneakers have rubber **soles** that usually provide great grips. Rubber wants to grip (grab) other surfaces thanks to a combination of uneven surfaces and softness. That's because **substances** with uneven surfaces tend to cling to other surfaces, and softness in those substances makes the **bond** even stronger. How? The softness encourages the rough edges to mold, or interlock, with the rough edges of the surfaces they're touching. That tendency for the two objects to adhere is **traction**. Traction is just what you need when you want to stop and go quickly.

So, why exactly did you slide? When you froze the sneakers, the rubber lost its softness. As a result, the sneakers lost their grip. In the future, store your sneakers in a closet instead, okay?

Smooth

Use two balls and some water to test how the fuzz factor affects swimmers.

What You Need

- Measuring cup
- Sink or outdoor area (that you can get wet)
- Smooth ball about the size of a tennis ball
- Tennis ball

What You Do

1. Fill the measuring cup with one cup of water. Pour the water slowly over the smooth ball. What do you observe?

2. Pour one cup of water slowly over the tennis ball. What difference did you see in the way the water ran off the smooth ball and the way it ran off the tennis ball?

What's Going On?

The smooth ball shed the water more quickly than the fuzzy tennis ball, right? The science that explains why also explains why competitive **swimmers** cover or remove all their body hair before a race. They aren't doing it to make a fashion statement—they're doing it to win races.

The swimmers are fighting **friction**, which is **resistance** (a slowing down) created when the swimmer's body moves against the water. Friction in **fluids** (like water and air) is called **drag force**. Drag force is created by **turbulent flow** of a fluid. Every little hair on your body makes its own pool of turbulence when you are in water—turbulence like you see around a rock in the river, when the water swirls around.

Multiply that swirling by thousands of hairs and you can understand why drag force makes a difference. (In swim competitions, a fraction of a second is the difference between **qualifying** for a race and watching the race from the bench.) So, swimmers want to create the opposite of turbulent flow, which is **laminar flow**. Laminar flow is when fluid travels in smooth lines around a surface. Shaved skin, like a smooth ball, creates more laminar flow than skin with hair.

What's even better than a close shave? Plastic-coated swimsuits made from the same type of material you see on speed-skater and track-cyclist bodysuits.

Wood Versus Metal

What You Need

- Baseball field or any other large open area
- One or more friends (You can also do this experiment by yourself, tossing the ball up or using a tee.)
- Wooden bat (Try to get a bat the same length as the aluminum one.)
- Baseballs or softballs (The more you have, the less often you'll have to run and get the ones you hit.)
- Aluminum bat

What You Do

1. Head to the field. Convince your friend that you need to hit first. (That's just because it's more fun to hit than pitch.)

2. Pick up the wooden bat and get in the batter's box while your friend gets ready to throw some pitches.

3. Swing until you've hit the ball about 10 times. (Only count the "good" hits that go farther than a bunt, okay?) Notice how far the good hits travel.

4. Switch to the aluminum bat and repeat step 3. How far did the balls travel this time?

5. Change places and let your friend repeat both parts of this experiment. Are her results the same as yours?

What's Going On?

CRACK! The sound of wood hitting a baseball is the one most people associate with the sport. But the truth is, except for when the pros are batting, the sound you really hear is the PING of **aluminum.** You've probably never hit with wood before in your life!

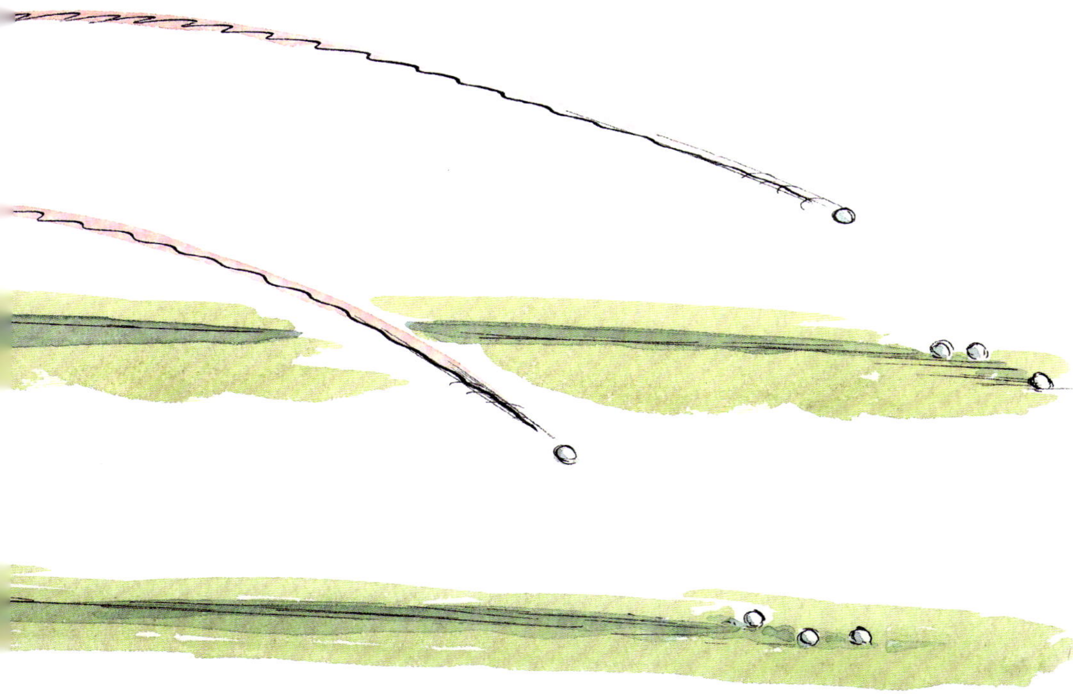

That's because in the 1970s most college, high school, and youth leagues switched to metal to save money. Aluminum bats don't break, so teams could keep using them for years instead of having to buy new ones every few days or weeks. That was good for bank accounts, but it was trouble for **pitchers.**

As you learned in this experiment, balls hit with aluminum bats go farther than balls hit with wooden bats. There are two reasons for this. First, aluminum bats are hollow and lighter even when they're bigger around. It takes less **force** (**energy** in motion) to swing them and you end up swinging them faster than you would a wooden bat. If the aluminum bat is bigger around, you also have a larger surface area to connect with the ball, which increases the odds of a hit. A faster swing means more energy is transferred into the ball you hit. So, the ball can travel faster and farther.

Second, since they're hollow, aluminum bats are slightly **elastic.** That means when a ball hits the bat, the bat **rebounds** most of the energy of the pitch. Yep, it's not all about power—the ball actually bounces off the bat! How much bounce? Well, scientists have suggested that if professional home-run hitters swung with aluminum, their hits would fly at least 30 feet farther.

Professional hitters are so good that every record in the book would get broken if they were using aluminum bats. That's why professional baseball leagues stick with wood.

Simple Spirometry

Test your lung power by blowing air into a bottle of water.

What You Need

- Large sink or outdoor area
- Measuring cup
- Empty 2-liter bottle (label removed)
- Marking pen
- Large mixing bowl
- Piece of plastic tubing (about 2 feet long)
- Friend
- An adult (optional)
- Paper and pencil

What You Do

1. Put the measuring cup and bottle in the sink. Fill the measuring cup with 250 milliliters of water and pour the water into the empty bottle. Use the pen to mark this level and write 250 next to the mark.

2. Fill the measuring cup again with 250 milliliters of water and pour into the bottle. This will make 500 milliliters of water in the bottle. Write 500 on the line. Repeat until you have marked all the way to 2,000 milliliters, or two liters. Then finish filling the bottle.

3. Fill the mixing bowl about half full and turn the bottle upside down in the mixing bowl. (Some water may leak out; that's okay.) Have your friend hold the bottle in place just off the bottom of the mixing bowl.

4. Thread one end of the tubing into the water and into the neck of the bottle. Take a few deep breaths and then blow once into the other end of the tubing. Watch as your air pushes the water out of the bottle. What measurement of water is left in the bottle? Write down that number.

5. Let your friend have a turn. Remove the tubing and refill the bottle. This time, you hold the bottle upside down in the bowl and let your friend blow. What was the measurement after her exhalation? Test an adult. How do the results compare?

What's Going On?

Have you heard of **spirometry**? Athletes who train for and compete in **distance events** sure have. Spirometry is the evaluation of how lungs function. You built and tested a simple **spirometer**—a device that measures **lung capacity** (how much air lungs take in and push out). Spirometers used by doctors and scientists are precise, measuring both how much and how fast you expire (exhale or blow air out). But your gadget worked well enough that you could see a difference in the results of your test subjects, right?

Your experiment revealed differences in lung capacity. These differences can be caused

by age, **genetics**, physical **conditioning**, and other **variables**. Your lungs transfer **oxygen** from the air into your blood, which then delivers oxygen to your muscles. If your muscles are not getting enough oxygen, they will lose power and not work as well. A lack of oxygen circulation is the biggest reason that athletes competing in **triathlons**, **centuries**, and similar races get tired. Anything athletes can do to increase their lung capacity is crucial to achieving their best performance. Lung capacity can be improved in several ways, including training with devices like the one you built.

Side Stitches

Do you ever get a stab of pain just below your rib cage when you are running or playing basketball? It might be a side stitch.

What causes the pain? Exercise physiologists don't agree, but one theory is that it's caused by the way you breathe while running or jumping. Breathing shallowly or irregularly and exhaling as you take a step might be pulling your diaphragm up while the rest of the organs in your abdomen drop with gravity. This could stretch ligaments, and repeated stretches might cause your diaphragm to seize upward—causing a stab of pain.

Exercise physiologists recommend that you avoid side stitches by breathing deeply and evenly during jarring physical activities. If you get a side stitch anyway, stop moving, press your hand on the painful area, and breathe evenly until the pain goes away.

Synchronized Skateboarding

Grab a friend and a couple of skateboards to test some push-and-pull activities.

What You Need

- 2 skateboards
- 2 helmets
- 2 sets of elbow pads
- 2 sets of knee pads
- 1 piece of rope
- Friend
- Level paved area

What You Do

1. Use caution as you do this activity and wear all your protective gear. You and your friend should place your skateboards head to head and sit on them so your feet are off the ground. Using your open palms, push off each other. What happened?

2. Now sit the same way but grab one end of the rope and have your friend grab the other end. Position yourselves so that the rope is stretched tight between you. On the count of three, you should both pull gently on the rope. What happens? Try it again, pulling with moderate force. What happens? Then take turns having each of you pull the rope gently while the other just holds on. What happens each time?

3. It's time for some experiments for just you and your skateboard. Stand on your skateboard with your feet hip-width apart and **perpendicular** to the direction the wheels roll. Get balanced so that you are standing still. Then slowly step off the front end of the board with the foot nearest that end. Now step off that same end with the other foot. What happened to the skateboard? Get on the board again, but this time quickly step off the same way—or jump. The skateboard should roll in the direction opposite your step or jump.

What's Going On?

This activity is all about how **momentum** (the **speed** and **mass** of an object in motion) can be shared between objects.

The objects in this experiment are you, your friend, and your skateboards. In each step of the experiment, the objects are interacting (part of a system). So, they can demonstrate the scientific principle known as the **conservation of momentum**. That principle states momentum present in a system is constant (maintains its total momentum despite changes in the system—including redirection). Keep reading! It will all make sense.

You and your friend provide the **energy** that puts you into motion. It didn't matter who pushed or pulled—you both moved. That's because you interacted and shared the momentum you created.

When you stepped off the skateboard from a standstill position, your movement was the force creating momentum. That momentum moved you in one direction—and the skateboard in the opposite direction. Because it had less **mass** than you, the skateboard was able to move farther before using up its share of momentum.

Understanding how momentum behaves can help skateboarders, surfers, and other athletes who ride sports equipment stay in control and stay safe.

It's a COG Thing

Your center of gravity (COG) is the key to balance. The trick to using it is finding it.

What You Need

- Chair
- Stopwatch or watch with second hand
- Friend
- Pillow

What You Do

1. Stand behind the back of the chair. Hold the stopwatch in one hand. Have your friend crouch down and grasp the front legs of the chair near the seat. Your friend will hold the chair down when you are on it so it doesn't fall over.

2. Set the pillow on the top of the chair back and lean over the chair so your stomach is on the pillow. (If the chair back is too tall for you to lean over, use a stepstool to reach it.) Now lift your feet off the floor and try to balance without holding on to the chair with your hands. For how long can you balance? Does it help if you stretch out your arms or legs?

What's Going On?

You found your **center of gravity**. That's the point in any **mass** (such as your body) where the weight is balanced. Being able to control this area is essential to controlling your balance—especially if you want to flip up, down, or all the way around like a **diver** or **gymnast**.

But controlling your balance isn't as easy as just finding your center. Did you notice how physically difficult it is to maintain balance when you are placing all of your weight in one spot on the top of the chair back? How long were you able to hold yourself in place? That's where **biomechanics** and **muscle** strength come into play.

Athletes from **skiers** to **cyclists** know the importance of **core strength**. Core strength is about all the muscles on the front, sides, and back of the waist. It's because the midsection is your center of gravity that those muscles are so important to any activity that requires balance. You use these muscles every day to roll out of bed, get up from a chair, walk, and more. (Test it: Sit in a chair, put your hand on your abdomen, and lift one leg straight out. Do you feel your abdominal muscles move? Try smoothly lifting both legs. Can you do it?) No matter what the task, people with more core strength and **conditioning** can move more quickly, more easily, and with less chance of injuries or soreness. In fact, the greater your core strength, the longer you can hold your balance in this activity.

Hot & Cold Bounce-Off

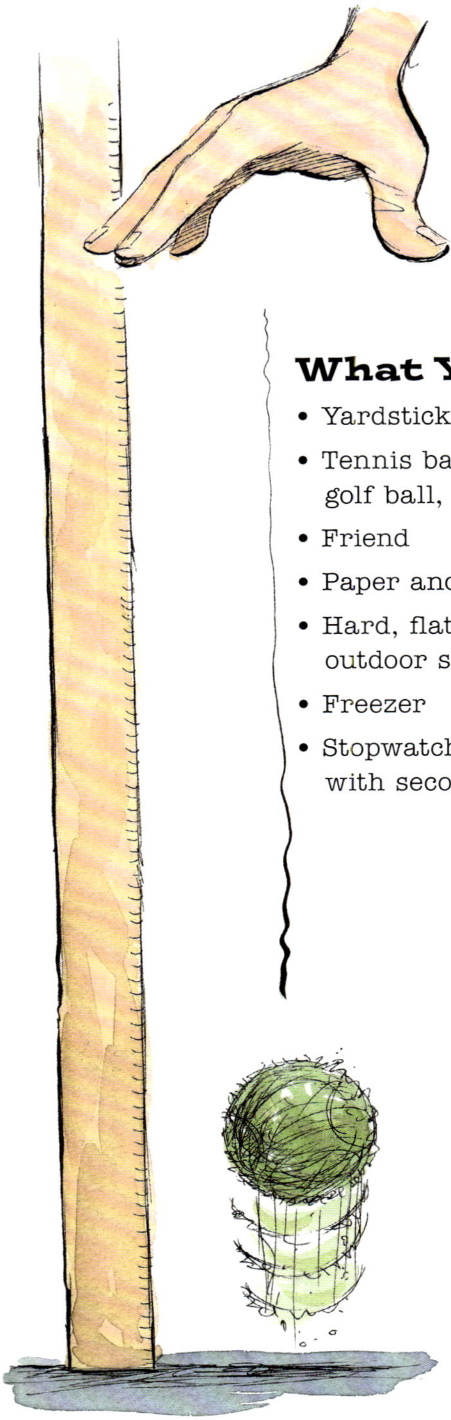

Test how changes in temperature affect the molecules in your tennis ball.

What You Need

- Yardstick
- Tennis ball, baseball, golf ball, and racquetball
- Friend
- Paper and pencil
- Hard, flat indoor or outdoor surface
- Freezer
- Stopwatch or watch with second hand

What You Do

1. Take your yardstick, balls, friend, and paper and pencil to the hard flat surface. Hold the yardstick **perpendicular** to the ground. Have your friend drop the balls, one at a time, from the same height. Look at the yardstick to see how high each one bounces and write the number down.

2. Put all the balls in the freezer and leave them in there for at least an hour.

3. Pull a ball out of the freezer, leaving the others to continue chilling. Repeat the experiment for each ball, but this time drop the balls and let your friend hold the yardstick. How high did they bounce this time? Have your friend record the results.

4. Let all the balls defrost at room temperature for an hour.

5. At the end of the hour, it's time to use the most complicated piece of equipment required for this experiment: your armpit. Take each ball and, one at a time, put it in your armpit for one minute and repeat step 1. How do these numbers match up with the first two sets of results?

What's Going On?

No, the last group of balls didn't bounce the highest because they were trying to get away from your stinky armpits. They bounced the highest because they were the warmest. And the second group of balls bounced the least because they were the coldest.

That's because balls are **elastic**, which means "capable of returning to an initial form after being subjected to conditions that changed their structure." One condition that changed them (temporarily) was being dropped. The other condition was being frozen.

When you release an elastic ball from your grip, the **force** of **gravity** pulls it to the floor. The **impact** is enough to make the ball flatten a little bit. But the ball, being elastic, wants to get back to its original shape. So it bounces up and away from the floor. No more flattened ball.

Here's where temperature comes in: Cold materials have cold **molecules**, and cold molecules don't like to move. A cold ball, therefore, will not flatten as much on contact. So there's less **rebound energy** and, therefore, less bounce. The flip side is that warm molecules like to move. So in cold weather keep your sports balls in the house, not the garage. Then they'll be ready to give you their best bounce.

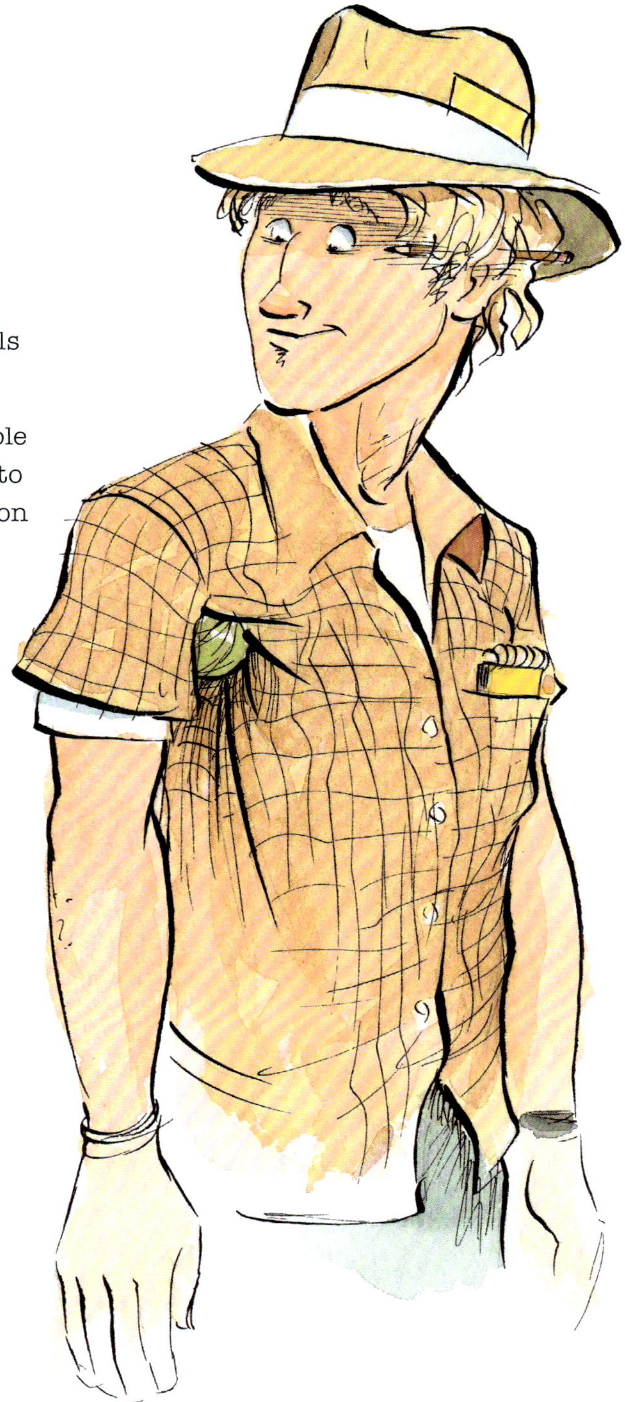

Spiraling Into Control

Experiment with different grips in search of the perfect pass.

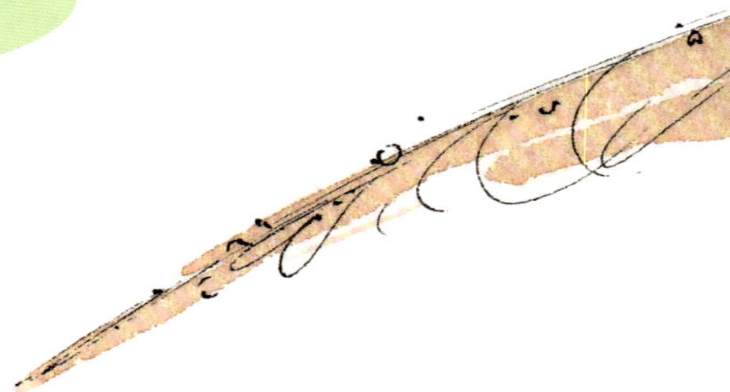

What You Need

- Football (foam or regular)
- Outdoor area
- Friend

What You Do

1. Stand 10 to 15 yards away from your friend. Grip the football with one hand, placing four fingers on the laces at the fattest part of the football and your thumb on the side or underside. See illustration above. (Where your thumb goes depends on the size of the ball and the size of your hand.) Then point the end of the football at your friend, pull your hand and the football back over the shoulder of your throwing arm, and throw the ball by hurling it in the air in a straight line toward your friend. Repeat this step a few times so you can see how the ball generally behaves when held this way. You want to see it travel in a **spiral.** (If you haven't thrown a football much, you may need to practice. Try varying the timing of your release of the ball and the amount of power you put into your throw.)

2. Move your fingertips back one lace and throw the ball a few more times. Notice how the ball behaves. Does it want to travel as far when you grip it this way? Do you have as much control over where it travels?

3. Repeat step 2, moving your fingertips back (toward you) one lace at a time until you get all the way to one pointy end. How did the behavior of the ball change as you changed the location of your grip?

4. Now put your hand back in the original position (see step 1). Instead of pointing the end at your friend, point the middle at her. Then throw the ball. How does it move?

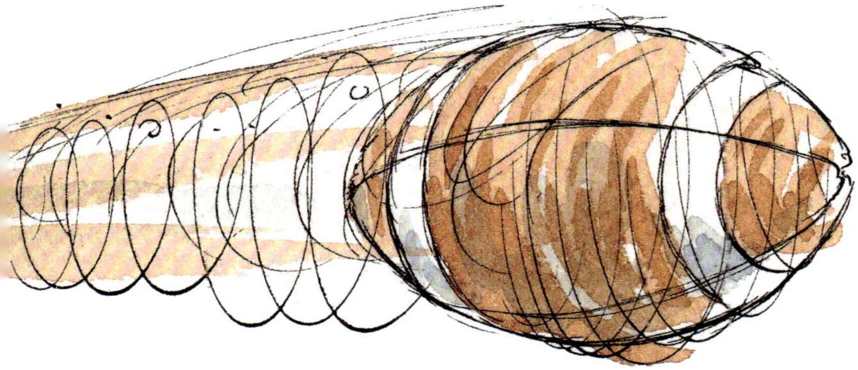

What's Going On?

Good **football quarterbacks** throw perfect passes. A perfect **pass** is one that reaches the **receiver** and still has plenty of **force** when it arrives. That makes it easy for the receiver to catch—the ball goes right to him, and it doesn't want to drop early or bounce around in the air.

The secret to throwing a perfect pass is controlling the ball's **velocity** (a combination of speed and direction). From a distance, it looks as if the football is magically sailing forward. But up close, you can see that the football travels in a spiral motion toward its target. A football is designed to want that spiral motion—and achieving the spiral motion gives you control of the velocity of your pass.

So what do you need to do? Grab the ball in the right place so that when you hurl it you see the spiral motion. To explain the spiral motion (the spin), you need to imagine a straight **line** is drawn from one pointy end of the football to the other pointy end. That line is called an **axis**, and the football wants to rotate (spin) around that axis. (The concept of spinning on an axis is a rule taken from **geometry**.)

In general, the grip described in step 1 is good for sending the ball forward in a balanced position so that it can rotate around that axis—instead of flipping or flopping in the air. (The perfect grip will be a little different for everyone—but it's usually near the fattest part of the ball.) Each time you moved your fingers farther away from the fattest part of the ball, you lost a little more control. The **speed** and **accuracy** of your passes decreased, right?

In step 4, did you notice a difference in how the side of the ball cut through the air compared to the pointy end of the ball? Because it's shaped in an **aerodynamic** point, the pointy end encounters less **air resistance** (slowing down caused by air). So even when you don't achieve the perfect spiral, the football will fly most easily when thrown pointy end first.

All About Angles

Cool off on a hot summer's day by discovering the secret to longer hits, kicks, or throws.

What You Need

- Garden hose with nozzle and handle to control the spray
- Protractor
- Friend
- Clothes that can get wet

What You Do

1. Hold the nozzle of the hose at shoulder level and keep it at that same height for every squirt. Hold the **protractor** in your other hand, level with the hose and **perpendicular** to the ground. Have your friend stand nearby, within range of the hose's spray. Start at zero degrees (horizontal) on your protractor and squeeze the handle all the way.

2. Now change the angle of the nozzle to 15 degrees and have your friend move to stay in the stream. Is he closer or farther away?

3. Repeat the activity, spraying the water at 30, 45, 60, and 75 degrees. Then turn the hose to 90 degrees (straight up). At what angle did the water travel the farthest into the sky? At what angle did the water travel the farthest forward?

What's Going On?

The water becomes a **projectile** after it leaves the hose. A projectile is anything launched that has no means of creating or supplying its own **force**. For instance, any ball used in a sport becomes a projectile. It's the player who supplies the force that launches the ball, with a kick, a hit, a throw, etc. (And sometimes the player becomes a projectile. See note on page 33.)

No matter what the projectile is, eventually forces in the environment make the projectile stop moving. The two primary forces are **gravity** (the natural force that pulls objects toward the Earth) and **air resistance** (a slowing down or change of direction caused by the force of air). Unless it's noticeably windy during this activity, air resistance is a minor factor. That leaves gravity.

So what's the best **angle** for delaying gravity's pull and getting the most height from your projectile? (Hint: the person holding the hose got soaked.)

Which angle sent the water the greatest distance forward? If you were trying to kick a soccer ball a long distance downfield to score a goal, that's the angle of travel you'd want. The water flew farther, but not as high at that angle, right? That's because what you lost in height you gained in forward distance. (The original launching force is the same regardless of the angle of the launch.)

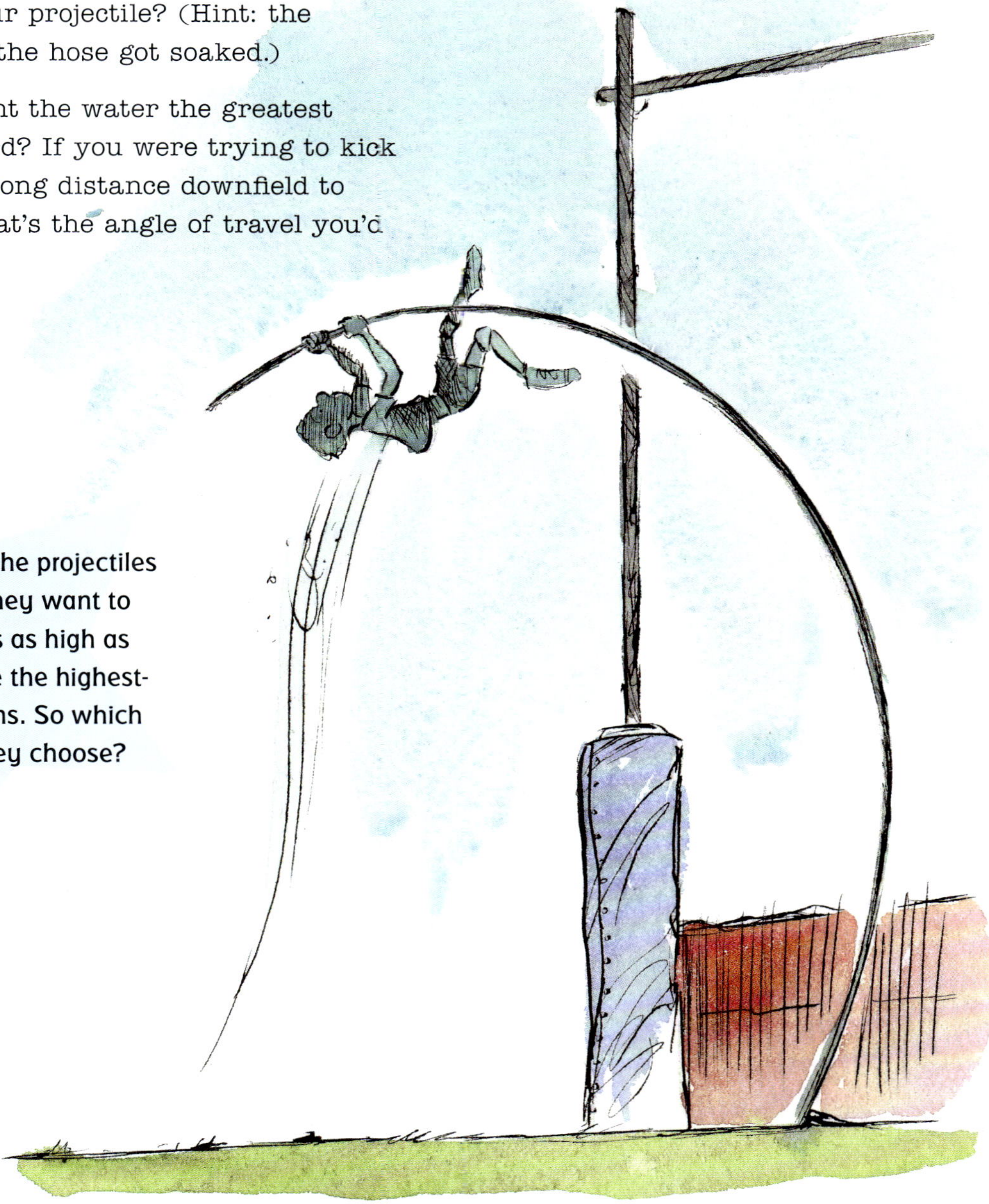

Pole-vaulters are the projectiles in their sport. They want to hurl their bodies as high as possible, because the highest-flying athlete wins. So which angle would they choose?

Watts Going On?

How much horsepower can you generate?

What You Need

- Paper and pencil
- Scale
- Flight of stairs
- Measuring stick that measures in centimeters
- Calculator
- Friend
- Stopwatch or watch with second hand

What You Do

1. Copy the Human Horsepower Calculation onto the piece of paper. You are going to fill in the blanks during this activity.

2. Step on the bathroom scale. Write down your weight in pounds, and then go to the flight of stairs.

3. Next, convert your weight into Newtons (a metric unit of weight, not the fig cookie). To do this, **multiply** your weight by 4.5. Write down the answer.

4. Count the number of steps from the bottom to the top. Make a note of that number. Measure the height of one step in centimeters. Multiply the step height by the number of steps. (Even if you are used to measuring in inches, you need to measure in centimeters for this activity.)

5. Divide the result of step 4 by 100. That new number is the total stair height in meters. Write down that number in the appropriate blank.

6. Hand your chart and your pencil to your friend, and have him stand at the top of the stairs with the stopwatch. You should move to the bottom of the stairs. When you're ready, run up as fast as you can while he times you. Have your friend write down your finishing time (in seconds).

7. Multiply your weight in Newtons by the total stair height. Divide that number by your time to determine your horsepower. What number in watts did you get? Repeat this activity so your friend can determine his horsepower, too.

What's Going On?

You used your body and brain to determine your **horsepower**. So, what's horsepower? First of all, **power** is a measure of the rate (what quantity in how much time) of doing **work**. Horsepower is a unit of measurement used to describe how much power is created by an engine, such as the engine in a motorcycle or a power tool. **Watts** are a measurement of the units of power used by inventions such as light bulbs and stereos when they operate.

If you got a number greater than 90, you could power a 90-watt light bulb in a lamp. If you created 746 watts you're officially a one-horsepower engine.

The more powerful you are, the more work you can do in a given time. But neither the fastest person nor the biggest person is necessarily the most powerful person. That's because power is a combination of ability to do work and the **speed** at which the work is done. Repeat this activity with friends and family and see how strong people and fast people compare.

Human Horsepower Calculation

Body weight in pounds = ________

Body weight in Newtons = ________
(multiply weight in pounds by 4.5)

Number of steps = ________

Height of 1 step in centimeters = ________

Total stair height in centimeters = ________
(multiply number of steps by height of one step)

Total stair height in meters = ________
(divide the total stair height by 100)

Climb time in seconds = ________

Horsepower in watts = ________
(multiply weight in Newtons by total stair height in meters, then divide by climb time)

Spitball

A little spit on a baseball makes a pitch tough to hit.

What you need

- Outdoor area (you'll be hurling baseballs, so stay away from windows)
- 2 baseball gloves
- Baseball
- Friend
- Petroleum jelly

What You Do

1. Put on your baseball gloves and throw the ball back and forth with your friend. Practice until you are throwing the ball well and it's going where you want it to go.

2. Now take off your glove and apply a little petroleum jelly to one spot on the baseball. Place your first two fingers on this spot, and throw the ball to you friend, just as you normally would. What happened?

3. Put on your glove and ask your friend to throw the ball the same way back to you—with her fingers in the spot of petroleum jelly. Watch what happens. What do you see?

4. Apply some more petroleum jelly and try putting your thumb on the spot as you throw. Does that make a difference in how the ball moves through the air?

What's Going On?

When you threw the baseball in step 1, it should have demonstrated a regular **trajectory** (flight path) and landed in your friend's baseball glove. That's because when you throw an ordinary ball, it follows certain rules that make its path predictable.

The ball becomes a **projectile** (an object that's launched into the air). A projectile is subject

to the **force** that launches it, plus the forces in the environment that act on it. Assuming you used the same basic **thrust** (forward push) for each throw, and the wind didn't change dramatically, the ball traveled the same way and landed in the same place on each throw.

But that's not what happened in steps 2, 3, and 4, right? What you and your friend threw then is called a **spitball**, even though the pitchers who used them didn't use spit most of the time. (Spit is mostly water, which tends to **evaporate** quickly. Pitchers preferred substances that stayed slippery, like **petroleum jelly**.) Your spitball's trajectory was unpredictable, zooming left and right and/or up and down. There are a couple of reasons why:

When you squeezed the petroleum jelly spot while making a throw, your fingers slipped and the ball squirted loose. This caused the ball to lose some thrust. That means less power to fight **air resistance** (a slowing down and change of direction caused by air). Air resistance wasn't a big deal for your ordinary throws, but now it makes the ball's surface spin less. The threads on the ball's surface are still moving, but slower than before, so even greater resistance is created between the threads and the air. Suddenly, the ball dances and flutters in the direction of the air—or multiple directions from crosswinds you may not even notice. The result may be an angry friend who had to duck to avoid your erratic spitball!

Spitball pitches were banned from professional baseball in 1920.

How Low Can You Go?

Discover why short people can have an advantage in sports.

What You Need

- Soft indoor or outdoor area with plenty of room to fall down safely
- Friend

What You Do

1. You and your friend are going to gently push each other, but someone might fall down so find a soft place to do this. Try a grassy, outside area. Start by facing each other.

2. Have your friend stand normally with his weight balanced between his feet. You do the pushing first. You DON'T have to push hard to see the results of this activity. Place your hands on your friend's shoulders and gently push. What happened?

3. Now place your hands on his hipbones. Push using the same amount of force you used on his shoulders. What happened?

4. Place your hands on his thighs and push, using the same force you used in steps 2 and 3. Is he still standing?

5. Switch places and repeat steps 2 through 4 so your friend can push you. Did you get the same results?

What's Going On?

The lower you positioned yourself, the easier it should have been to push your friend. Was that true for your friend when you were the one being pushed? People have a **center of gravity** that is located around their belly button. Your center of gravity is the point where the majority of your weight is centered over the **force** of the earth pulling it down (**gravity**). **Balance** is basically your body's ability to keep a foundation under this weight so you don't topple over.

When you pushed your friend around his shoulders, you were above your center of gravity. It wasn't easy to push him, was it? That's because your friend was able to keep control of his center of gravity by leaning into you.

But the lower you get before pushing, the easier it is to knock somebody over. That's because once you get below a body's center of gravity—which you did when you pushed on your friend's hipbones—his body can't find balance. When it can't find balance, the body loses its battle with gravity and falls down.

Low is the way to go to keep an advantage in most sports, whether you are trying to make a **tackle** or are making a play in a **one-on-one**, close-contact sport. For instance, in **basketball** you can **box out** another player. No, you don't hit him: Boxing out is turning your back to your **opponent** when you have the ball, bending your knees to crouch, and using your rear end to push him out of the way as you move down the court.

Players who excel in the positions of **noseguard** in **football**, **prop** in **rugby**, or who make good **wrestlers** aren't necessarily tall athletes. In fact, a lack of height can actually give them an advantage—if they use it correctly. That's the reason why football coaches always say, "the low man wins."

Racing Arms

Do you need more than strong legs for a fast run?

What You Need

- Level racetrack
- Chalk (optional)
- Friend
- Stopwatch or watch with a second hand
- Long bungee cord (optional)
- Paper and pencil

What You Do

1. Find a racetrack with start and finish lines, or mark lines with chalk. Get warmed up by jogging around the track.

2. Have your friend get ready with the stopwatch at the finish line while you toe the start line. When she says go, take off and run as fast as you can, with one restriction: you can't move your arms. This will be a lot harder than you think. That's why you may want to use the bungee cord to tie your arms down. Record your time.

3. Switch places with your friend and time her. Record her time.

4. Drink some water and catch your breath. When you're ready, run the course again. Pump your arms as much as you like. What was your time in this run? Give your friend a turn. Did her time improve?

What's Going On?

Freeing your arms should result in a faster run. That's because you need your arms free for good running **form** (technique).

How fast you run depends on your **stride frequency** and **stride length**. Stride frequency is how many steps you take, which depends on how fast you can get your feet up and down. (You can improve your stride frequency through **conditioning** routines such as skipping rope.) Your stride length is how much distance you cover with each step. Pumping your arms with each step (which is how people naturally move) lengthens your stride. That's because as you drive your elbow up, it causes your knee to lift higher. When the knee goes higher, it takes longer to get back to the ground. So you cover more distance with each step.

Good form also helps athletes perform better in sports that require just a few steps of running, such as volleyball, long jumping, and vaulting.

Curveballs, Dropballs, and Screwballs

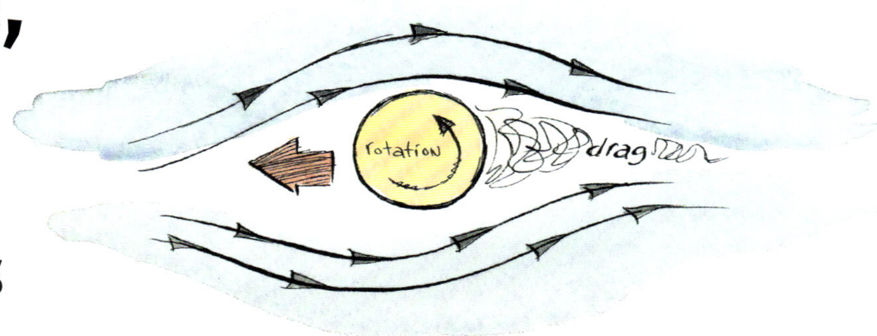

Launch a ping-pong ball to re-create classic baseball pitches.

What You Need

- Cardboard wrapping-paper tube
- Ping-pong balls (that fit inside the tube)
- Small piece of sandpaper (optional)
- Glue (optional)

What You Do

1. Hold the tube like you'd hold a baseball bat, gripping it near one end with one hand.

2. Use the other hand to drop a ping-pong ball into the tube and quickly swing the tube as if you were swinging at a fastball. You might have to try a few times to get the ball to come out.

3. What happened? Try different angles of your swing and observe how the ball flies each time.

4. For even more spin on the ball, glue the sandpaper to the inside end of the tube and try the swings again.

What's Going On?

The ball spins as it comes out of the tube. You put a spin on it by controlling the change in its direction (flinging it out of the tube). The sandpaper should increase the amount of spin, because sandpaper is rough and creates **friction** when the ball strikes it. Did you notice that the greater the spin, the greater the curve in the ball as it flies? Also, by changing the direction of the swing, you changed the direction of the curve.

But what makes the ball curve once it's in the air? The curve is created by differences in the direction of the air after it passes over the ball, which is called the **Magnus effect**. As the ball spins in the air, one side is pulling the air over it and causing the **wake** behind the ball to bend to that side. The other side is stopping the air, causing that air to slow down and not bend as much. This change in wake direction creates **lift**, which causes the ball to move in the direction that's offering less **air resistance**. Lift can occur in any direction, so a drop is actually pulled down by lift.

Go Figure

Grab a chair that spins and two soup cans to test how figure skaters can increase speed in a spin.

What You Need

- Chair that spins freely
- 2 soup cans (full)
- Friend

What You Do

1. Grab one soup can in each hand and sit in the chair. Stretch your arms out to your sides, parallel to the ground.

2. Start spinning the chair by pushing off the floor with your feet. (Your friend could also help by pushing you around by your feet.)

3. When you are spinning fast, pick up your feet. Have your friend count how many revolutions you make before the chair comes to a stop.

4. Now get the chair going at the same speed, and cross your arms tightly to your chest. How many times did you go around?

What's Going On?

You spun more times with your arms crossed, didn't you? That's due to a scientific principle called **angular momentum**. Angular momentum is created by the combination of **angular speed** (how fast you spin) and **radius** (the distance from the center of the circle you spin in to its edge).

Let's assume the **speed** of your spins (outstretched arms and crossed arms) were similar. Then we can assume that your angular speed was consistent. So what changed was your radius. How?

When you stretch out your arms, you create a large radius. When you cross your arms over your chest, you create a smaller radius. Crossed arms translate into faster spins and more spins.

That's why **figure skaters** end their routines with a spin that rotates faster as they pull their arms closer to their bodies.

High Jumping High Jinks

To reach for the sky, start by getting a little closer to the ground.

What You Need

- Friend
- Yardstick

What You Do

1. Stand with straight legs and jump as high as you can. Have your friend use the yardstick to measure how far your feet got off the ground.

2. Now bend your knees a little and jump as your friend measures the height.

3. For your last jump, bend your knees fully before you spring up. How high did you go this time? How did the three jumps compare?

What's Going On?

It takes a lot of **energy** to jump, and your legs generate the most energy when they use as many **muscles** as possible. The two biggest muscles in your body are your quadriceps (thighs) and your gluteus maximus (butt). The more you bend your knees, the more muscle fibers you can use. And the more muscle fibers you use, the more upward **force** you generate.

Did it ever seem you were bending too much and your jump was short? Your leg muscles might be unfamiliar with this kind of jumping, so they aren't ready to fully **flex** and **contract**. (With **training**, they'll learn how to respond.) Or maybe your **balance** was off, not your bend. Your balance is based on how you position your **center of gravity** (your midsection, right around your bellybutton). Keep your center over your feet as you bend, instead of tipping back or tipping forward. You should be able to take advantage of even the deepest knee bends.

Belly Flop Science

Use diving techniques in a pool to determine the best position to slow a skydive.

What You Need

- Adult permission to dive
- Swimming pool (filled with water, of course)
- Swim clothes
- Friend

What You Do

1. NEVER dive into a shallow pool. Stand on the edge of the pool where the water is the deepest. Dive in with a normal hands-first position. Do this a few times. Have your friend watch to see how much of a splash you make, and how quickly you submerge. Also, notice how it feels to enter the water this way.

2. Dive in a feet-first position. Again, have your friend observe how much of a splash you make and how quickly you sink. How do you feel yourself moving through the water?

3. Dive into the pool in the **belly flop** position (Warning: This dive will hurt a little.) Have your friend observe the splash and how quickly you submerge. How did that dive feel?

What's Going On?

Have you seen **skydivers** as they plummet towards the Earth? They fall as fast as 200 miles per hour. But most skydivers want to go slower than that, to stay in control and enjoy the ride. Your diving experiments should have revealed what position creates the greatest **resistance** to invisible physical units called **molecules**—resistance that can slow a skydiver's fall.

You can't see them without a **microscope**, but everything is made up of molecules. You can't touch molecules, but you can sometimes feel the **pressure** they put up against your moving body. When you dived into the pool hands-first, you should have created the least splash, had quickest submersion, and felt the smoothest entry. That's because your body adopted an **aerodynamic** shape, making it possible to strike relatively few water molecules as you entered the pool.

Jumping in feet-first was less aerodynamic, so you had more area of your body coming into contact with more water molecules. So you created more splash, had a slower submersion, and felt yourself hitting more water.

Belly flopping offered the entire front side of your body to make contact with many more water molecules. And you felt the resistance they offered you in return, right? It hurts when you belly flop in water because water molecules are densely packed. **Density** allows for more molecules in less space, which creates greater resistance. Resistance is what makes things feel hard.

How does this relate to skydiving? Your dives demonstrated that making contact with lots of molecules at once slows you down. Using the belly flop position, a skydiver has the best chance of slowing his fall. Luckily, air molecules are not dense. So belly flopping through the air doesn't hurt.

Off-Road Riding

Ride on- and off-road to see and feel the difference.

What You Need

- A mostly flat, unpaved biking trail
- A flat, paved biking trail or safe road
- Your bicycle (an all-terrain bike is best)
- Helmet
- Bicycle odometer with timer
- Paper and pencil

What You Do

1. If your trails aren't mostly flat, that's okay. The point is to have two trails that are similar. So, choose two totally flat trails, or two somewhat hilly trails.

2. Calibrate the odometer according to its directions. You'll use it to measure the distances you ride and to time yourself.

3. Take a test ride on the unpaved trail to map out a 1-mile course. Notice the surfaces and features of the trail, such as, "smooth dirt for ½ mile, loose gravel for ¼ mile, slight incline near the end." Record your findings.

4. Take a second ride on the unpaved trail, timing yourself. Bike at a moderate pace. Record your time. Also note how comfortable you were during the ride. Did you bounce around much? Did you lose balance?

5. Take a test ride on the paved trail to map out a 1-mile course. Note of the trail conditions. Record your findings.

6. Time yourself as you bike on the paved trail. Ride at the same pace as before. Record your time and your notes about how the ride felt. Which trail did you finish quickest?

What's Going On?

Differences in the surfaces you rode on, as well as the **terrain**, all played a role in your **speed** on each trail. Your time on the paved trail was quickest, right?

That's because a smooth surface creates less **friction**, allowing the wheels on your bike to roll smoothly. Even when you're facing a tough uphill, a smooth surface free of debris is easier to climb. A rough or sinking surface, such as a trail with loose rocks or mud, offers greater resistance. Varying surface conditions also make it harder to handle your bike, which can also slow you down.

Spin-Ups

A football's unusual shape lets it jump from a spin to a stand.

What You Need

- Football

What You Do

1. Lay the football on the ground. A smooth surface works well. Use both hands to grip it on each end and spin it at slow-to-medium speed. What did the ball do?

2. Then, spin the football as hard as you can. If you do it right, something amazing will happen. (Hint: keep trying until the ball stands up by itself.)

What's Going On?

You may have seen professional **football** players make a football spin and stand up by itself in the **end zone** after a **touchdown**. Were you able to do the same in this activity?

Because of its unusual shape, a football has two **axes**. (No, not the things you chop trees down with—axes is the plural of the word **axis**.) An axis is an imaginary **line** between two **points** on an object, around which an object can rotate (spin). This imaginary line always runs through the center of the object. In order to spin, an object needs to be symmetrical (balanced on each side of its center line).

A round ball can have many axes, which are the same lengths. A football has only two axes: a short axis and a long axis. The short axis goes from side to side in the centermost part of the ball. The long axis runs from pointy end to pointy end. Objects with axes of different lengths are most stable when spun around the longest axis. That's why when you spun the ball slowly it wobbled around on its short axis, but when you got it going on its long axis it stood up and twirled like a **ballerina**.

Give Me a Holler

Does making a racket while you use your racquet make you a stronger player?

What You Need

- Court or outdoor area
- Tennis racquet
- Tennis balls
- Friend with racquet (optional)

What You Do

1. Wind up and smack a few tennis balls as far as you can with your racquet. (This is where it would be good to have a friend. If you're alone and retrieving the balls yourself, there isn't quite as much incentive to go for distance.)

2. Try again, but this time you're going to make some noise. Yell as loud as you can as you strike each ball. Try a variety of yells—think grunts and groans, not screams. Did the balls fly farther when you made some noise?

What's Going On?

Did yelling or grunting help the ball sail much farther. Scientists who specialize in grunting (yes, there really are scientists who specialize in grunting) say that engaging your lungs and windpipe can give players more **power**. But scientists argue about the reason for the increased power. Some theorize that grunting or yelling causes a surge in **adrenaline**, so you are literally pumped up with **energy**. Others surmise that the added noise makes you concentrate more. Then you engage more **muscle** fibers toward the task at hand, striking the tennis ball with as much strength and skill as possible. Whatever the reason, athletes in many sports can't seem to keep quiet when they play. At least the noise they make could be making them play better!

In Position

Find your best biking position by competing against yourself in a coasting contest.

What You Need

- Long straight, sloping (downhill) road with no traffic
- Chalk
- Helmet
- Bicycle
- Friend
- Stopwatch or watch with second hand
- Paper and pencil

What You Do

1. Use the chalk to mark start and finish lines on the road. Your racecourse should be roughly as long as a football field.

2. Ready to race? Sit as upright as possible on this ride, with both hands on the handlebars and both feet on the pedals. Have your friend start the stopwatch as soon as you roll across the start line. Remember, no pedaling. Coast all the way to the finish line. Record your time.

3. For the second **time trial**, lean toward the handlebars. Don't pedal. Coast all the way to the finish line. Record your time.

4. For the last trial, lean toward the handlebars so that your face is only a few inches away from them. Also, pull your elbows tight to your sides. Have your friend time your coast through the course.

Racers want to minimize air resistance. You can see their experiments in the funky design of helmets for the Tour de France, low-riding racecar bodies, and clingy plastic-coated bodysuits.

What's Going On?

You recorded your quickest time when tucked in the last riding position, right? Competitive **cyclists** call that the **tuck position**. They adopt that pose whenever they want to shave seconds off their race time. The tuck position is **aerodynamic**, which means it reduces your body and bike's **resistance** to the air you sail through as you ride.

But why is the air resisting you in the first place? Because **friction** (a slowing down caused when two objects move against each other) exists even between invisible air **molecules** and the molecules that make up your body. The greater your contact with the air, the more **collisions**, and the more you get slowed down.

Disc Tennis?

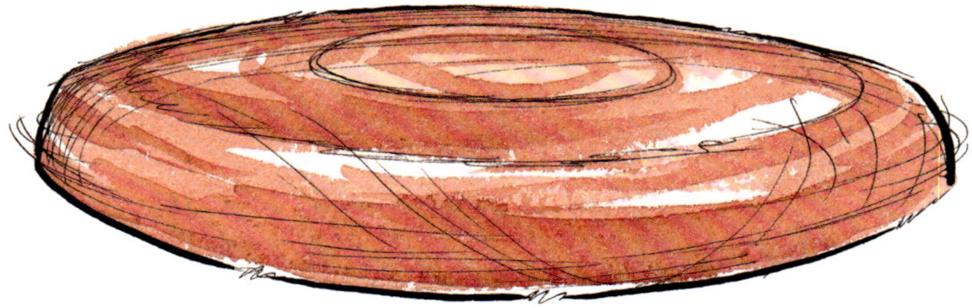

Step up from just tossing a flying disc with this experiment for forehand and backhand passes.

What You Need

- Flying disc (you can use a Frisbee or any other brand disc)
- Friend (or two or three)

What You Do

1. The **backhand** is the first throw most people learn, so you might already know it. Place your thumb on top of the disc and your index finger along the rim. To make the throw, extend your arm and flick your wrist as you let go of the disc. The goal is for the disc to fly forward while staying parallel to the ground. The key elements of the movement are **spin** (created by flicking the wrist) and **speed** (created by extending the arm quickly). Once you get the hang of it, practice your backhand throw several times. How far is it sailing?

2. Now try the **forehand**. Grip the disc with your thumb on top and your ring finger and middle finger on the inside of the rim. Extend your arm slightly and flick your wrist forward as you release the disc. Your palm should be facing up when the throw is done. Once you get the hang of it, practice your forehand throw several times. How far does it go? Is the distance greater or less than your backhand throws?

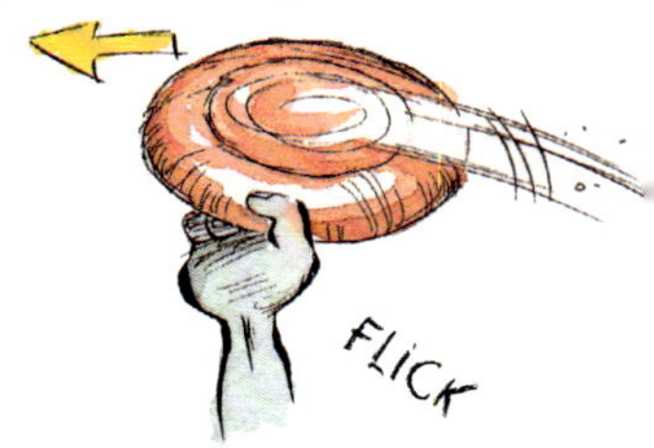

What's Going On?

The backhand throw went farther, didn't it? That's why a backhand is perfect for **teeing off** in **disc golf** or **kicking off** in **ultimate**. The forehand throw can't cover the same distance, but it takes less time to throw a forehand. So a forehand is great for tight **passes** in a game of ultimate.

How is it that a **disc** can sail through the air so easily, pretty much any way you throw it? There are two reasons: the disc's shape lends itself to flying, and air tends to want to lift and carry the disc—a tendency explained by a scientific law called **Bernoulli's principle**.

A disc is an **airfoil**, with a shape and function similar to an airplane wing. An airfoil is designed to cut through **air resistance** (a slowing down caused by air). And an airfoil is also designed to create **lift** from the air flowing around it. Lift literally pushes the airfoil up.

How? As the disc cuts through the air, some air is pushed below the disc. That pushed air has a higher **pressure** (upward force), and lifts the disc. Meanwhile, the air above the disc is lower in pressure and therefore creates a downward **force**. This downward force keeps the disc from flying straight up.

So why does the air tend to carry a disc—especially when you throw the disc perfectly level? That's where Bernoulli's principle comes in. It says that a rise in pressure in a flowing **fluid** (air, water, etc.) is accompanied by a decrease in speed. It also says that the opposite is true: lower pressure is accompanied by an increase in speed. A disc thrown perfectly level and with enough force balances these changes as it flies.

Inflation Lessons

What bounces higher: a pound of weight or a pound of pressure?

What You Need

- Basketball, soccer ball, or volleyball
- Air pump
- Inflation needles to fit each ball
- A hard surface (to bounce a ball on)
- Scientific scale (or any scale that measures in grams)
- Paper and pencil

What You Do

1. Put the needle in the ball at the inflation opening and let out as much air as you can.

2. Remove the needle. Drop the ball from chest height. How high does it bounce? Then weigh the ball on the scale, and record both how high it bounced and the weight.

3. Put the needle back in the ball, attach the needle to the pump, and pump in three strokes of air. Then remove the needle and drop the ball again. How high did it bounce? Now re-weigh the ball. Record your findings.

4. Repeat step 3 two more times, or until the ball is hard when you press on it with both hands after inflating it. What was the final bounce height of the ball? What's the final weight of the ball? How did the bounce and the weight change each time you inflated the ball?

What's Going On?

The **weight** of the ball didn't change much, right? That's because air doesn't weigh much. But the ball with the most air in it should have bounced the highest. That's because you were adding **pressure**, not pounds, to the ball.

Pressure is a measure of how much **force** is pressing on an area. The air **molecules** you pump into the ball supply the force that presses against the inside of the ball. That's why a flat ball begins to take shape when you add air. The more air molecules there are, the more force they can exert. Because a ball is **elastic**, when it hits anything it deforms briefly and then springs back into shape. A higher pressure ball bounces higher because all those molecules inside are pushing the ball back into its round shape.

Got Sole?

The tops of shoes are what people see, but the bottoms are what do the work.

What You Need

- Piece of wood for a ramp (at least 3 feet long)
- Dress shoe
- Basketball shoe
- Running shoe
- Protractor
- Paper and pencil

What You Do

1. Place the dress shoe parallel to the length of the board at one end of the board and slowly lift that end of the board while leaving the other end on the floor or ground. Find the angle at which the shoe begins to slip and make a measurement with your **protractor**. Write the number down.

2. Now turn the dress shoe so that it is perpendicular to the board and repeat. What was your angle this time?

3. Let's try the basketball shoe next. Measure the angle at which it just begins to slide and write the value down. Turn it and try again. Repeat for the running shoe. Which shoe slid at the smallest angle? Which slid at the highest angle? Did turning the shoes make any difference?

What's Going On?

The dress shoe slid at the least **angle**—slipping easily down the board, right? That suggests how easily it would slide over the grass or dirt if you were trying to outrun a **defender** or get to a **ground ball**. Running shoes and basketball shoes, on the other hand, are designed to have **soles** that grip. That helps you move quickly and stay moving, while also being able to stop quickly.

Which slid at a lesser angle, the running shoe or the basketball shoe? Typically, the **resistance** and **rate** of slide will be similar. That's because **basketball** is played on a smooth court and has a lot of grip on the smooth board. **Running** is usually done on rougher surfaces such as a rubber track, asphalt, or trail, so the shoe soles have more varied surface designs that create **traction**. Traction will keep you on your feet, instead of sliding on rocks, and the soles will all but stop any slide on the board.

The keys to choosing the right athletic shoe are determining how much friction you'll be fighting and how much stability you need.

Strikes & Spares

Go bowling in your yard and throw strikes at spare bottles.

What You Need

- Measuring tape or yardstick
- String or rope (or use boundaries such as the edge of the driveway or a hedge)
- Outdoor area
- 10 empty plastic soda bottles (Raid the recycling bin. Bottles must all be the same size.)
- Soccer ball
- Friend
- Old bowling ball (Get permission to use the bowling ball.)
- Garden hose and outdoor spigot

What You Do

1. You're going to make a bowling alley. Use your measuring tape and string to mark a lane 1 yard wide and about 10 feet long.

2. Fill the bottles with water and tighten the caps. Place the 10 bottles in a pyramid shape (one in front, two in the second row, three in the third row, and four in the last row) at one end of the lane.

3. Now bowl a few frames with the soccer ball. Take turns with your friend, with one of you bowling and one of you setting up the bottles that get knocked down. Try to keep the ball rolling at the same speed each time.

4. After a few frames, use the bowling ball and try the experiment again. Were the bottles easier or harder to knock down? Remember to take turns being the bowler and try to keep the speed the same each time.

What's Going On?

In this competition, the bowling ball should have demolished the bottles—and given you better results than the soccer ball. Do you know why? It has everything to do with the weights of the moving objects (the balls) versus the weight of the **stationary** objects (the bottles), and the nature of a **collision** (when objects hit each other). The force of a moving object, called **momentum**, is the key to collisions.

Momentum is easy to see but can be hard to explain. The amount of momentum an object has depends on the object's **mass** and **speed**, or **force** and **time** (the time in which the force acts on the object). In this activity, the bowler's **muscles** supply the force and time. You tried to roll the balls with similar force and time, so we can focus on figuring out the differences in the mass (weight) and speed of the balls as they roll.

You should have seen that giving a lightweight soccer ball a roll created momentum. Did you also notice that giving a heavy bowling ball a roll created a lot more momentum? Also, you should have seen the heavier ball pick up speed faster than the lighter ball. Meanwhile, the bottles just stood there—until struck by either ball.

Here's where the science of collisions comes in. When objects collide, the object with more momentum typically transfers that extra momentum to the weaker object. That transfer usually causes a movement or redirection of the weaker object.

Did the soccer ball have enough momentum to knock over some or all of the bottles? That depends on how much force you put into the roll and the weight of the bottles. If you couldn't knock them down, pour out some of the water and/or try rolling the ball harder. The bowling ball should have easily knocked over the bottles. Its weight was much greater than the bottles', and the strength of your roll should have helped create lots of momentum.

Lean on Me

Discover why where you lean when you change directions can make the difference between making a turn and falling flat.

What You Need

- Bike helmet
- Bike
- Pylon, bucket, or anything else you can put on the ground that will stay in place
- Paved, flat area such as a driveway
- Friend

What You Do

1. Put on your helmet and take your bike, pylon, and friend out to the driveway. Set the pylon down where there's plenty of room for you to ride around it in a complete circle.

2. Get on your bike and set a course for the pylon. When you get to it, circle it once just to practice. Next time, try to go around it as tightly as possible, as if it were a corner. Try to keep your bike straight up and down as you change direction—no leaning. (You won't be able to do it. You'll either keep going straight or you'll fall down. So be careful!)

3. Now have your friend ride around the pylon, but she shouldn't try to keep the bike or her body straight. She should just ride. After a few circles, have her pedal faster. What happens each time she makes the turn?

4. Try it again yourself, this time without the bike. Jog around the pylon, and then run around it full speed. What happens to the position of your body? The same thing that happened when your friend rode the bike, right?

What's Going On?

For much of your life you've done this leaning action without thinking because your body knows what it needs to do in order to avoid falling down. But does your brain? It's about to learn.

When your body leans, it's instinctively working to create something called **centripetal force**. Centripetal force pulls a rotating (spinning) object toward a center or **axis**. Unlike the natural **force** of **gravity**, centripetal force is not always present. An object—someone or something—must apply it.

For instance, if you hold on to a bar on a merry-go-round as it spins, that handhold creates a force—centripetal force—and you are pulled into the spin and ride safely. But if you are on a merry-go-round and don't grab on, the force of the spin will make you fly off. (That's due to **centrifugal force**, which is a reaction to centripetal force. It pulls objects away from the center of a spinning object.)

If centripetal force isn't ever present like gravity, and you didn't reach your hand out to hang onto the pylon, what applied the centripetal force? Centripetal force is created two ways on your bike, so you've got the tires and road plus yourself to thank for avoiding a wipeout.

The tires and the road create **friction** (powerful resistance from objects rubbing against each other). It's enough **force** to create centripetal force, which you assist by leaning in. (And leaning in just feels right because it helps you maintain your **balance**.)

When you watch a sport like **motocross** racing, in which competitors on **motorbikes** race and do tricks on a round track, it's easy to see just how important leaning and centripetal force is to some athletes.

Sweet Spot

Use a bat or racquet to find the best place to strike the ball.

What You Need

- Wooden bat and baseball, or tennis racquet and tennis ball
- Colored tape
- Friend

What You Do

1. With one hand, hold the bat so that it is **perpendicular** to the ground. Your hand should be on the handle, and the barrel should be hanging down. Tap the baseball on the bat starting near your hand and working your way down, an inch at a time. What did you feel when you tapped near the handle? Was there a spot where your hands didn't feel much vibration?

2. Repeat again until you find a spot where your hands don't feel much vibration. Mark this spot with colored tape. This should be the sweet spot, but let's go outside and see for sure.

3. Have a friend lob balls to you and purposely hit a few off the handle or the end of the bat, away from the tape mark. What do you feel and hear? How are the balls flying? Now repeat, but try to hit on the sweet spot. What did you feel and hear this time? How are the balls flying? Repeat the experiment with the other optional equipment. (For instance, use a tennis racquet and ball instead of a bat and baseball). How do your results compare?

What's Going On?

When you hit a ball with a bat or a racquet, the **impact** creates **vibrations** that travel in **waves** up and down the length of the object. But there's a point, called the **node**, where the vibrations meet and cancel each other out. That's the **sweet spot**, which every bat- or racquet-swinging athlete wants to locate.

Steps 1 and 2 were all about finding the sweet spot, while step 3 tested how that spot performed. Were you able to find the spot by feeling the vibrations? When you hit the balls using that spot, did you notice the ball sailing farther through the air? Could you hear when you hit the sweet spot? With a wood bat, you can easily hear the difference between a ball that's been struck with the sweet spot and one that hasn't. The sweet spot creates a loud CRACK sound.

As you probably knew even before doing this activity, it's not much fun to hit a ball with the end of the bat or the handle. The vibrations sting your hands, right? Even worse, when you miss the sweet spot, the bat's energy is lost to those stinging vibrations instead of going into the ball. So not only are you hurting, you've probably hit a weak **pop-up** somewhere instead of an out-of-the-park **home run**.

Professional baseball players take years to learn how to consistently hit the ball off the sweet spot. Some experts say accomplishing that might be the most difficult feat in all of sports.

Why Bats Sting—and Sing

If you've ever played a xylophone, you probably weren't thinking much about baseball. But the truth is, a single bar on a xylophone actually behaves just like a bat—right down to some sweet music.

When you strike the bar of a xylophone with a mallet, it vibrates (shakes in a gentle, regular rhythm) around the two spots where it is attached to the frame. Those spots don't move—only the bar moves. It is the vibrations of the bar between those areas that create sound. The vibrations are energy in motion. It takes energy to make the bar move, and you supply the energy by striking the bar.

A wooden bat behaves the way. You put energy into a bat by swinging it, and when it makes contact with a baseball, some bat energy transfers and is used to send the ball into the air. The collision of bat and ball also causes the bat to vibrate between two points, just like the bar on a xylophone. When you hit the ball with just the right spot, the bat sings out with a CRACK. That crack is the most beautiful sound a hitter can hear.

Saddle Up

Get comfortable in your seat for your fastest ride.

What You Need

- Short racecourse (your driveway, your backyard, or a street without car traffic)
- Chalk
- Helmet
- Bicycle (one that's your size)
- Bicycle smaller than your regular bike (optional)
- Tricycle (optional)
- Stopwatch or watch with second hand
- Adjustable wrench
- Ruler
- Paper and pencil
- Friend (optional)

What You Do

1. Go to the course and use the chalk to mark start and finish lines. (Or you can choose an obvious stationary object, such as a tree or mailbox.) You can use the stopwatch yourself, but it's probably easier to have a friend stand at the finish line and time you.

2. If you have a tricycle, climb on at the start line. (If you don't have a tricycle, go to step 3.) How do those bent knees feel? At the count of three, pedal as fast as you can to the finish line while your friend times you (or you time yourself). Write down the result.

3. Now go back to the start line and get on the small bicycle. (If you don't have one, go to step 4.) Repeat the experiment. What was your time?

4. Take your regular bike to the start line. With the wrench, lower your saddle (this is what cyclists call a seat) to the lowest possible height. If you have a quick-release saddle, lucky you. Just pull out the release, lower the saddle, and push the release securely back in place. When you're ready, ride your regular bike to the finish line and write this time down. Are you seeing a pattern?

5. Go back to the start line and use the wrench to raise the saddle one inch for each ride you make, timing yourself each time until the saddle is so high your foot can't reach the pedal. What saddle height allowed you to pedal the fastest? What height felt the most comfortable to you?

What's Going On?

Some people say that the **bicycle** is the most efficient man-made machine. The only fuel it needs is your strength, and using a bicycle doesn't create any pollution. This activity should have shown you that a good fit on a bike is essential if you want to use your **energy** wisely.

Biomechanics is the study of how **muscles** generate **force**, and biomechanics is important in **cycling**. If your **saddle** is too low, you aren't able to activate all the **muscle** fibers in your legs because they don't get to extend as far as they should for an efficient stroke. Did you get a "just spinning your wheels" feeling when you rode on a too-short saddle? This wastes energy and you can't go very fast.

If your saddle is too high, however, your hips have to rock to reach the pedal. Did you feel yourself having to slightly readjust to pedal when you were on the too-high saddle? That wastes energy, too.

For the easiest ride possible, your leg should be almost completely straight when the pedal is at its lowest point. This allows you to engage the maximum amount of muscle fibers. You should also be able to achieve the fastest race time when your saddle is just the right height. So saddle up the right way to maximize your **power** and ride to the front of the pack.

Catch Me If You Can

Giving is the key to catching a water balloon—without getting wet.

What You Need

- Large outdoor area
- Water balloon
- Swim clothes (or clothes that can get wet)
- Friend

What You Do

1. Grab a friend and fill a few balloons with water (some for the experiment and some to throw later during the inevitable water-balloon fight).

2. Stand about 6 feet apart and gently toss the water balloon to your partner and have her toss it back. After you each make a catch, take one giant step backwards and gently toss the balloon again. Keep moving farther apart until somebody gets an unexpected bath. Repeat again with another balloon. Can you keep the balloon from exploding when you catch it? How? How far apart can you get until it does? (Pick up the rubber pieces of the broken balloons and put them in the trash.)

What's Going On?

Did you figure out the secret to staying dry? The key is to "give"—meaning to move your hands in the direction the balloon is falling as you catch it.

Here's how "giving" works: the product of **force** and **time** is called **impulse**. Impulse is needed to stop any moving object. By increasing the time it takes the balloon to stop, you decrease the force that the balloon feels as it stops moving. So the balloon is less likely to burst.

In sports, if you give with a ball as you catch it, you can control it by lessening the force. But you won't be able to catch the balloon forever if you keep getting farther away. That's because the balloon must be thrown harder the farther it must go. Eventually there will simply be too much impulse required to stop it from breaking.

Reading Your Reaction

How quickly your body responds depends on how much your brain has to think.

What You Need

- Ruler
- Friend

What You Do

1. Hold a ruler between your thumb and index finger so that it dangles **perpendicularly** to the ground. Make sure the other end is between the thumb and index finger of your other hand. Let the ruler go and then quickly grab it again with your other hand. How far did it fall? (Look at the ruler to see.)

2. Now have your friend hold the ruler and we'll try it again. How far does the ruler fall before you can catch it when he lets it go? Try it again and see if you get faster with practice.

3. Use the table below to calculate your reaction time. Switch places and let your friend try. Why were you faster when you dropped the ruler?

Distance	Reaction Time
5 cm (2 inches)	.10 seconds
10 cm (4 inches)	.14 seconds
15 cm (6 inches)	.17 seconds
20 cm (8 inches)	.20 seconds
25 cm (10 inches)	.23 seconds

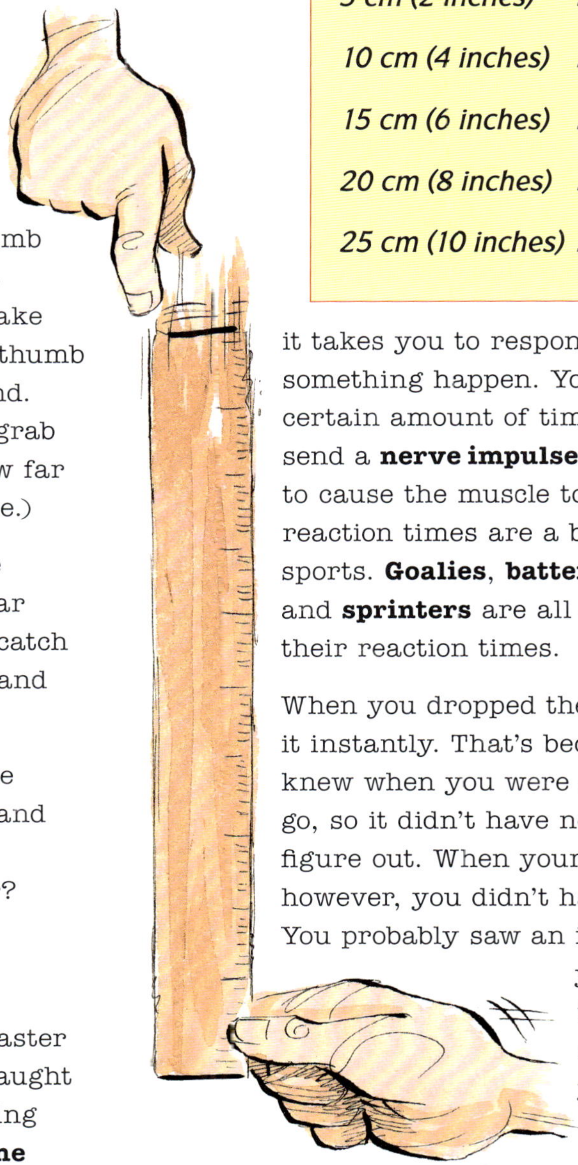

What's going on?

Did you figure out why you were faster when you dropped the ruler and caught it? The explanation lies in something called reaction time. That's the **time** it takes you to respond when you see something happen. Your brain takes a certain amount of time to see the act and send a **nerve impulse** to your **muscle** to cause the muscle to **contract**. Good reaction times are a benefit in most sports. **Goalies**, **batters**, **tennis** players, and **sprinters** are all only as good as their reaction times.

When you dropped the ruler, you caught it instantly. That's because your brain knew when you were going to let it go, so it didn't have nearly as much to figure out. When your friend dropped it, however, you didn't have that advantage. You probably saw an improvement as you practiced a few times, but you still can only improve your time a little.

Ramp It Up

Experiment with energy using a marble and a cardboard ramp.

What You Need

- Cardboard
- Scissors
- Tape
- Marble

What You Do

1. Use the cardboard, scissors, and tape to build a ramp like the one you see in the illustration.

2. Drop the marble onto the ramp at one end so it can roll down. Watch how it moves.

3. Repeat the activity, dropping the marble from different angles and heights. What happens each time?

What's Going On?

If you dropped it from a great enough height, the marble **caught air**—flying up and away from the ramp before touching back down and rolling in the opposite direction. What kept it going? The seesaw relationship of **potential energy** and **kinetic energy**.

Before you release the marble, it has potential energy. That's **energy** stored in the marble because of it's position (in this case, its height) and the pull of **gravity**. (An object at greater height experiences greater pull, resulting in more stored energy.)

As the marble rolls down the ramp, the marble's **mass** (weight) is in motion. This causes it to build **speed** and kinetic energy (energy present in a moving object). At the lowest part of the ramp, the marble's potential energy is gone—it's all changed into kinetic energy. Kinetic energy powers the marble's roll up the opposite side of the ramp. By the time the marble has risen its highest, the kinetic energy has all become potential energy. This back-and-forth energy transformation continues, with the marble losing a bit of energy as **heat** each time it rolls up. The marble's rising and falling finally ends when all the energy is used.

So how does a **skateboarder** keep going when he rides a ramp? First, his bodyweight provides lots of potential energy to get him started. Then he keeps going by generating **momentum** (an amount of forward movement). A skateboarder does this by using his **muscles** and the **angle** of his body to change his speed and direction.

Fits Like a Glove

Wood is good for learning how to field ground balls.

What You Need

- 2 pieces cf 1 x 4-inch wooden boards, about as long as your hands
- Baseball or softball
- Friend

What You Do

1. Hold a piece of wood in each hand and bend ycur knees to assume a **fielding** position. Have your friend roll the ball at you. Try to catch it with the pieces of wood. This may take some practice, so don't get discouraged. If you're having trouble, here's a tip: as soon as the ball hits the wood, gently draw your hands—and the wood—back toward your body.

2. Gradually increase the distance the friend is away from you and have him increase the speed of the ball. Were you able to keep scooping up the ball?

What's Going On?

You were able to scoop up the ball with the wood if you pulled the ball toward you, in the direction it was already going, right? You might have heard the term "soft hands" when referring to an **infielder** in **softball** or **baseball**. This activity teaches you how to develop soft hands.

The rolling ball has a certain amount of **momentum**, which describes how fast it's moving as a result of its **mass** and the **velocity** at which it travels. When you catch a ball, you are trying to get rid of all the momentum because you to want control where it is in space. (Ideally, you want the ball to stay in your glove until you throw it.) So unless you want to force the ball to stop dead in its tracks and absorb all that energy quickly, you need to take your time to stop it. You absorb momentum by using an **impulse**, which is the combination of the **force** and the time taken to stop it. Moving the blocks of wood gives the ball more time to use up its momentum and slow down. When you **trap** a **soccer** ball, the same concept causes the ball to stay at your feet.

Go Slow

Challenge your friends to the slowest bike race ever.

What You Need

- Level road without traffic
- A couple of friends
- A bike for each person
- Stopwatch or watch with second hand (optional)

What You Do

1. Pick a starting point and an ending point. Use two mailboxes, two light poles, or the entire length of your street. You are going to race each other—with a twist. Last person to the finish line wins! This is a balancing activity that will teach you a little about bikes.

2. A few rules: you must be headed toward the finish line at all times, you can't touch your feet to the ground or lean on anything (like a mailbox). No tricycles or training wheels allowed. You can also use a stopwatch to time each other on the same bike. Try all the different bikes to see if some bikes are better than others at going slowly.

What's Going On?

The tricycle would always win (if allowed in the race). That's because a tricycle doesn't require that its rider maintain her **balance**. The tricycle does it for you. Those three wheels ensure that the tricycle stays balanced, whether you are sitting still or pedaling—fast or slow.

When riding a regular bike, the trick to staying up and winning the slow race is to keep your balance. To do that, you have to keep your **center of gravity** directly above the middle of the bike. That's hard to do, unless you are moving. So you probably ended up pedaling only when you had to—when you were about to fall over!

Bend With It

The key to landing is learning to relax.

What You Need

- Stairs or stepstool

What You Do

1. Step up on to the first stair. Jump off to the ground, keeping your legs as straight as possible. What do you feel?

2. Now, jump down again, but bend your knees a little as you hit. Was that easier?

3. Finally, jump but bend your knees all the way. How did that feel compared to the other jumps?

4. For an optional activity, jump onto a carpeted floor and roll as you hit (like your favorite action hero).

What's Going On?

Athletes who play sports that involve hitting the ground learn the science behind this activity early in their training. **Gymnasts** are taught to roll as they hit the gymnastics mat. **Running backs** learn to relax as they're **tackled**.

Volleyball players learn to slide as they **dig** for a ball. The jumping you did in step 3 should have felt the most comfortable.

That's because when you increase the **time** it takes something to stop, you decrease the **force** that object feels while stopping. Force is what got the object moving in the first place. In the case of jumping off a step, the force is a combination of your bodyweight (your **mass**) and **gravity** (a natural, constant force that pulls things down). Bending your knees as you land should give you just enough time to decrease the force.

Air bags in a car work because of the same concept: they don't stop a person from slamming forward in a head-on collision, but they might slow the person down enough to prevent serious injury.

I Feel a Draft

Use a candle's flame and a pie pan to see the air stream that racers like to ride.

What You Need

- Candle
- Matches (and adult permission to use the matches)
- Aluminum pie pan

What You Do

1. Light the candle and hold it in your right hand. Hold the pan in your left hand. Keep the objects shoulder width apart. Move both of your hands to the left at the same speed. Observe the candle flame. Which way does it point?

2. Now, move the pie pan to about 3 centimeters from the candle and repeat. Which way does the candle flame point this time?

3. Put out the candle.

What's Going On?

Danica Patrick and **Carl Edwards** must have done this activity when they were children, because they use it a lot as professional **racecar** drivers. It's a demonstration of **aerodynamic** principle called **drafting**, which can be done with cars as easily as candles.

The candle's flame is blown with the wind when your hands are apart, but when your hands are close together the flame stays upright or actually bends towards the pan. As the pan moves, air going around the pan creates a swirling air current called a **vortex**.

This vortex spins quickly and, according to a scientific rule called **Bernoulli's Principle**, fast air creates lower **air pressure**. This leads to less air resistance (a slowing down caused by air pressure). So, if you are directly behind another racer—it doesn't matter if she's a **runner**, **driver**, or **cyclist**—you feel less air resistance. You can go faster because you are being slowed down less by the air.

But that's not all that happens. You'll be pulled along with the front racer by the air, giving you a free ride. How's it a free ride? You don't have to expend as much **energy** (in this case, power from **muscle** energy or from burning gasoline in your car's engine) as the person or object whose air pulls you.

Drafting for Two

Because of their aerodynamic design, racecars can create a kind of drafting that pulls both vehicles forward as they speed around the racetrack. The pull can even make both cars travel at a greater speed than their engines are able to create.

Even though they might team up to benefit from drafting, the second car is waiting for the right moment to pull ahead. How does that work? If the second driver times it correctly, he builds **momentum** with each lap. He relies on that momentum to fling him ahead when he moves out from behind the leader. At the same time, he relies on a change in air resistance (caused by the end of the drafting) to pull the leader back. Combining strategy and science like that wins races.

Slap Shots

Hockey sticks bend and flex.
What does flex do for your shot?

What You Need

- Wood hockey stick, graphite hockey stick, and aluminum hockey stick or 3 hockey sticks with different flexibility ratings
- At least 3 pucks (the more pucks you use, the less time you'll spend fetching them)
- Ice rink
- Goal (optional)
- Hockey skates
- Protective hockey gear
- Paper and pencil

What You Do

1. Stand at one end of the rink with your hockey sticks. You'll be hitting the pucks to the other end.

2. Choose a hockey stick. Take two practice hits, and then hit the puck as far as you can. Record your result on paper by making a diagram to show how far the puck traveled.

3. Repeat step 2 with the other hockey sticks, one at a time. Record your findings. Which hockey stick helped you hit the longest shot?

What's Going On?

You just tested how much distance you get from **hockey sticks** with different amounts of flex (ability to bend). The reason flex matters is that an object that can flex has a lot of **potential energy**. Potential energy is energy or power that an object has stored because of its structure (or its position in a electric, magnetic, or gravitational field). In the case of a hockey stick, it's the structure (the way it's shaped and made) that gives it potential energy.

When you are making a pass or taking a shot in a hockey game, more flex can give you more energy—energy that sends the puck farther. Next thing you know, you've

nailed a **hat trick** and your team tackles you to celebrate. (You might want to ask if next time they'll hoist you on their shoulders, or something else that's less painful than being jumped on by a hockey team.) The weight and the size of the stick and your strength also matter. When you think you've become a stronger hockey player, repeat this test and see if your preferred hockey stick has changed.

No hockey sticks?

You can demonstrate the science of this activity another way, using a yardstick, a coin, and a table. Set the yardstick on the table so that you can see the measurements. Make the stick hang off the table by 5 inches. Set the coin on that end of the yardstick. Holding the stick on the table with one hand, use the other to bend the end of the stick toward the floor, and then release. How high does the coin fly?

Move the yardstick so that more or less of the stick hangs off the table, replace the coin, and use the same amount of bending pressure each time. (The overhanging section of yardstick is working like the hook part of a hockey stick.)

The coin flips highest into the air with what length of yardstick overhang? That's the point at which you found the most potential energy.

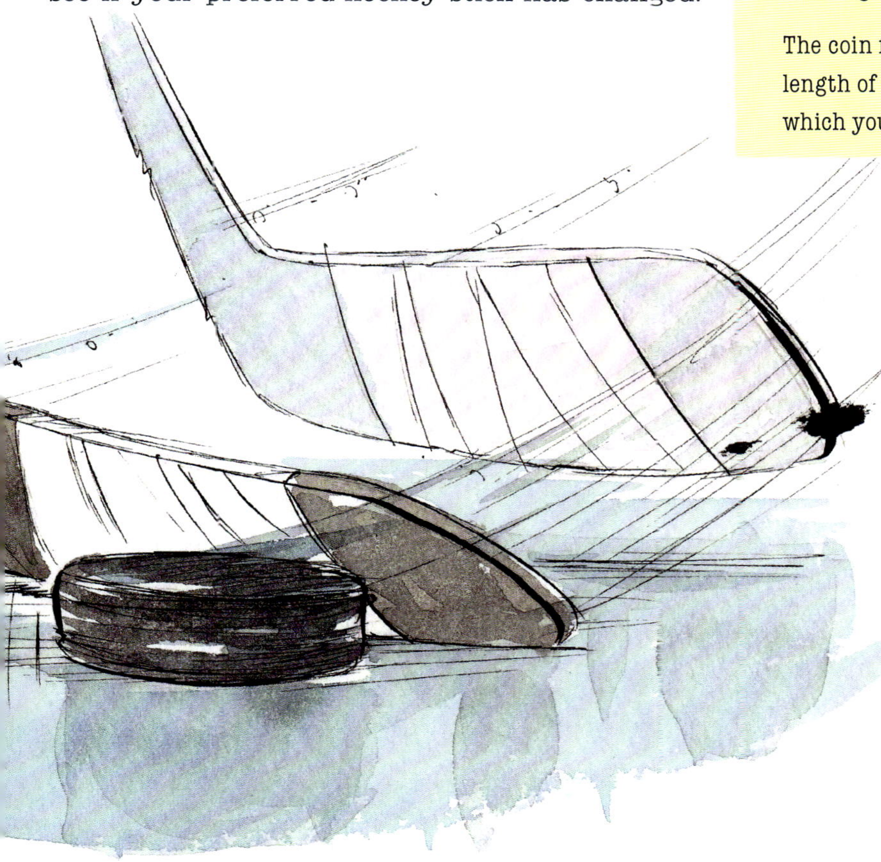

All Geared Up

When you want more "get up and go," nothing gives it faster than the gears on your bike.

What You Need

- Bicycle (must have several gears and different speeds, like a ten-speed road bike or a mountain bike)
- Chalk
- Friend
- Tape measure or yardstick

What You Do

1. Make sure your bike is in the lowest possible gear (with the chain on the smallest front sprockets and largest back sprocket). With chalk, mark a spot on the road right where the front tire meets the road.

2. With your friend helping you balance on the bike, take two complete revolutions of the pedals before coming to a complete stop. Use the chalk to mark where the bottom of the front wheel is on the road now and use the tape measure to figure the distance between your two marks. How far did you go?

3. Now try the next three (higher) gears and record your results each time. Which combination moved you the farthest? Which moved you the least? Which was the hardest? Which one was the easiest?

What's Going On?

You've probably felt the difference when pedaling your bike using different gears. Now, you've actually measured the difference. When you pedal a bike, you are using **energy**. Your goal is to use this energy wisely. All gear combinations give you a different **mechanical advantage**.

Mechanical advantage is a measure of the gear's ability to change the **force** put into it (from your leg power) and or the distance traveled. A higher gear offers a higher mechanical advantage because it can make the bicycle roll farther using the same energy.

Different gear combinations will help you in different situations, such as going up a hill or riding on a flat surface. The large front sprocket will help you zoom down the flat road the fastest, but the small front sprocket helps you climb hills.

Have you seen pictures of the first bicycles, the ones that had a huge front wheel? In those bikes, the mechanical advantage came from the **diameter** of the wheel. The larger the wheel, the greater **speed** and **power** the biker had. It took a lot more strength to pedal those early bikes, though.

Hang Time

Hang in the air and wave to the crowd before you sink your next basket.

What You Need

- Basketball goal (adjustable, preferably)
- Basketball
- Friend
- Stopwatch

What You Do

1. Your goal is to stay in the air as long as possible. Have your friend time you with the watch. From a standing position, jump straight up as high as you can.

2. Take a running start and jump as high as you can while your friend times you. Try again, but this time jump out more than up. What was your best time in the air?

3. Let your friend try. It's your turn to time him. Did either of you stay in the air for an entire second?

4. Lower the basketball goal to the lowest height and see if you can dunk away the day.

What's Going On?

Were you able to increase your **hang time**? If you made adjustments to your **speed** and **angle**, you should have noticed a difference.

As you were jumping, you became a human cannonball. You were a **projectile**, launched by the **muscles** in your legs. Projectiles don't choose how high they fly. That's determined by the **launch**. How did you control your launch? By choosing your speed and your takeoff angle. Those factors combined to determine where you went once you got into the air.

Greater speed yields greater height. A running start puts greater speed in your jump than jumping up from a standstill position. So a running start should send you higher into the air.

But what about angle? You probably earned your best hang time when you jumped straight up. That's because more of your leg force was driving straight up, putting up the best fight against the **force** of **gravity** (the natural force that pulls everything down). **High jumpers** go almost straight up because they want height to clear the bar. **Basketball** players who are near the basket and want to score jump straight up. Players with a lot of reach and a good jump can sail to the basket from several feet away.

Did it amaze you that you probably never spent more than one second in the air? Only the world's best athletes can do that. Test it yourself: watch the best players on a basketball team and time them with a stopwatch. (Don't time the slow-motion replays. Just the live play!)

Don't Stop Now!

If you liked this book, check out *Smash It! Crash It! Launch It!* We build balloon dragsters, launch water balloons with slingshots, and more.

Do you prefer science with more bubble than BANG? Read *Cool Chemistry Concoctions: 50 Formulas that Fizz, Foam, Splatter & Ooze.*

Astound your friends and family with science tricks that work like magic with the help of another one of our books, *It's Not Magic, It's Science!*

There's also a book for your animal friends: *Pet Science: 50 Purr-fectly Woof-Worthy Activities for You & Your Pets.*

Glossary

Adrenaline. To prepare for action, your body secretes this hormone, increasing your heart rate and blood pressure.

Aerodynamic. Designed to create the least air resistance. Aerodynamics is the study of the movement of gases and the way objects interact with air.

Airfoil. An object designed to create lift as air flows around its surface.

Air resistance. A force created by friction that slows down (or stops) an object's motion through air.

Aluminum. A lightweight metal that is easily shaped.

Angle. A shape formed by two lines or planes that start at the same point.

Angular momentum. A property of spinning objects. The object's angular velocity, mass, and how the mass is distributed determine its angular momentum.

Angular velocity (angular speed). How fast an object is spinning, measured in revolutions per minute.

Axis. Imaginary line around which an object rotates. Axes is the plural of axis.

Backspin. A spin that slows a moving ball down or causes it to travel in another direction.

Balance. A state of equilibrium, meaning opposing forces balance out each other and stability is attained.

Ballerina. A female dancer in a ballet.

Baseball. A game played with a ball and bat by opposing teams of nine players. Also, the ball used in a baseball game.

Baseball diamond. The shape created by four bases that baseball players run around to score points.

Basketball. A game played by opposing teams of five players who try to throw a round ball through a raised basket.

Batter. A player in a game of baseball or softball who takes a swing at a pitched ball with his bat.

Belly flop. A painful way of jumping in the water and landing flat, belly first.

Bernoulli's principle. A scientific law about the velocity and pressure of a moving fluid. It states that when the speed of a fluid increases, its pressure decreases. It is named after the scientist, Daniel Bernoulli of Switzerland.

Biomechanics. Body movements and the forces acting on the body. Also, the study of this.

Bond. A substance or force that holds things together.

Bowl. A natural or man-made bowl-shaped area.

Bowler. A person who plays a game involving knocking down 10 pins by rolling a ball down an alley.

Box out. To use your body to keep a player away from the ball (or basket) by putting yourself between them.

Bunt. A batted hit in baseball or softball that intentionally lands between the pitcher and the catcher.

Catch air. To go up with enough energy to leave the ground.

Center of gravity. An imaginary point where an object's weight is concentrated. Also called center of mass.

Centrifugal force. An apparent force that seems to pull spinning objects away from the center.

Centripetal force. What causes an object to move in a circle, directing it toward the center of the circle.

Centuries. Races that cover one hundred miles.

Chemistry. The study of matter's properties, structures, and reactions.

Collision. To come together with direct impact. When objects collide, they exchange energy and momentum.

Conditioning. The process of taking part in regular exercise, stretching, and other activity in order to develop your body for a specific sport or an active lifestyle.

Conservation of momentum. The total momentum of objects interacting remains constant.

Constant. A quantity that does not vary.

Contraction. Shortening and thickening, as seen in muscles when they cause limbs to move and bend.

Core strength. The physical condition of the torso muscles.

Curveball. A pitched ball that veers to the left or right.

Cyclist. A person who rides or races a bicycle, motorcycle, or similar vehicle. Generally, cyclist refers to a bicycle rider.

Defender. Anyone playing a defensive position, trying to prevent the opposing player or team from scoring.

Density. The compactness of a substance, determined by how many units are packed in a space.

Dig. To move quickly (often down close to the ground) to be in position to return a ball.

Disc golf. A game based on the rules of golf, in which flying discs are thrown into targets.

Distance events. Long races that require more endurance and stamina than speed.

Diver. An athlete who dives into water, typically from a high platform into a pool, often while doing acrobatic moves.

Drafting. To position close behind a fast-moving object to take advantage of the reduced air pressure and forward suction the object produces.

Drag force. A force parallel to the surface of a moving object that pushes against the forward motion, slowing the object's movement.

Drag racing. Racing two cars, beginning from a standstill and relying on rapid acceleration.

Driver. A professional pilot of a vehicle, such as a racecar.

Dropball. A ball that falls unexpectedly fast after being hit or thrown, making it hard to hit, catch, or return.

Drop shot. A ball drops quickly after crossing the net.

Edwards, Carl. American racecar driver.

Elastic. As in elasticity: the ability of a solid object to return to its original shape.

End zone. In football, the area at either end of the field, between the goal line and the end line.

Energy. The ability to do work or activity. Energy can be transformed, expended, or stored.

Evaporate. To change from a liquid into a vapor (gas) at a temperature below the boiling point.

Exercise physiologist. A professional who uses physical activity to help people improve and maintain their health and fitness or train as athletes.

Fielding. Catching or taking control of a moving ball.

Figure skater. An athlete who performs a type of ice skating with choreographed jumps, spins, and other graceful or acrobatic moves.

Flex. To bend, or to tighten up your muscles.

Fluid. Anything that flows, including gases, water, and oil.

Football. Team sport played with an oval ball in which the ball is carried or thrown (American football). Team sport played with a round ball in which the ball is kicked (international football).

Football field. A 100-yard long playing area (American football). A 110-120-yard long playing area (international football).

Force. Something that causes an object to move, change speed or direction, or deform in shape.

Forehand. A move made with the palm of the hand moving forward, such as a forehand tennis stroke.

Form. Technique.

Friction. Resistance between moving objects. Friction slows down (or stops) one or both objects.

Genetics. Inherited physical or behavioral traits.

Geometry. The science of shapes in mathematics.

Goal. The line, zone, basket, or net that players try to get a ball into or past to score points.

Goalie. The player whose job it is to guard the goal by blocking scoring attempts by her opponents.

Gravity. The natural force of attraction exerted by a mass, such as Earth. Gravity draws objects toward Earth's center.

Gymnast. An athlete who competes in a sport requiring great strength, flexibility, and acrobatic technique.

Hamm, Mia. American soccer player.

Heat. Energy contained in objects because of moving particles. "Lost" energy is typically converted into heat.

Home run. When a baseball player bats a ball such that he is able to run around all of the bases.

Horsepower. A unit of power equal to 745.7 watts. The power needed to lift 550 pounds one foot in one second.

Impact. One object striking another.

Impulse. Force multiplied by time in a collision.

Indoor sport. A game that's always played inside.

Inflate. To fill something with air to make it swell.

Inflation. The act of inflating something.

Invert. Turn upside down.

James, LeBron. American professional basketball player.

Knuckleball. A pitch that doesn't spin but moves in unexpected ways.

Laminar flow. The orderly movement of a fluid along a straight line, typically at a high velocity.

Lift. The forces perpendicular to the surface of an object that is traveling through air. Lift normally pulls the object upward.

Ligament. Fibrous, stringy tissue that connects bones or holds organs.

Line. A figure formed by two points.

Lob. To throw, hit, or otherwise move a ball in a high arc.

Long jump. Players run and then jump, competing to travel as far as possible before landing.

Lung capacity. The amount of air your lungs can hold.

Magnus effect. The perpendicular force that causes a spinning object to curve in its path.

Mass. A body of matter, or how much matter is in a body.

Microscope. A scientific instrument used to magnify objects to a size where you can more easily see them.

Mechanical advantage. How much a machine multiplies the force put into it.

Molecule. The smallest particle of a substance, usually composed of two or more atoms.

Momentum. A measurement of the motion of a body, equal to the product of its mass and its velocity. Momenta is the plural of momentum.

Motion. Also called movement. The act or process of changing position or place.

Motocross racing. Off-road motorcycle racing.

Mountain bike. A rugged bike designed for riding off road.

Mountain biking. Riding a mountain bike on dirt trails or other unpaved terrain.

Muscle. Tissues that contract to help the body move.

Newton's first law. A body at rest tends to stay at rest, and a body in motion tends to stay in motion at a constant speed in a straight line, unless acted upon by a force. Also called the law of inertia.

Newton, Isaac. The mathematician and scientist who developed the three laws of motion.

Newton. A unit used to measure force, equal to the force needed to accelerate a one-kilogram mass one meter per second.

Newton's laws of motion. See Newton's first law, Newton's second law, and Newton's third law.

Newton's second law. The rate of change of an object's accleration is proportional to the force acting on it, and the direction of the change is the direction of the force.

Newton's third law. For every action (application of force) there is an equal and opposite reaction (application of force in the opposite direction).

Noseguard. A defensive player who keeps blockers away from his team's linebackers.

Olympic. Relating to the Olympic Games, an international sports event begun in Olympia, Greece, in 776 BC.

One-on-one. A game in which two individuals are the only opponents playing against each other.

Opponent. A player on the other team.

Out of bounds. Beyond set limits for a playing field.

Oxygen. An element essential for life in most organisms. Oxygen fuels athletic activity.

Particles. Very small pieces of matter.

Pass. To throw or otherwise give a ball to a teammate.

Patrick, Danica. American racecar driver.

Perpendicular. Intersecting at right (90°) angles.

Petroleum jelly. A goo that can be applied to pitch a spitball.

Physics. The study of matter and energy and their interaction.

Physiology. The study of living things, their parts, and functions.

Pins. The targets bowlers try to knock over.

Pitcher. In baseball, the player who throws the ball from the mound to the batter on the opposing team.

Point. The unit for keeping score in sports.

Pole vaulter. An athlete who uses a long, flexible pole to hurl (vault) herself high into the air to sail over a bar (without knocking down the bar).

Pop-up. In baseball, a ball hit high in the air, making it easier for the opposition to catch.

Power. A measurement of the ability to do work. Power is a combination of how much work is done (the rate) and how quickly it's done (the speed).

Pressure. Force applied or distributed over a surface area.

Projectile. An object that is launched by an outside force acting on it.

Prop. An offensive position in rugby.

Protractor. A tool for measuring angles. To use, place its hole over the point of an angle. Place the zero on the protractor along one of the angle's sides. The number on the protractor where the other side of the angle intersects the protractor's curved edge is the degree of the angle.

Pylon. A short tower that marks a turning place.

Qualifying. Competing successfully in rounds that will determine who plays the final round.

Quarterback. The offensive leader in football, who throws the football, hands it off, or runs.

Radius. A line between the center of a circle and its circumference.

Rebound. To gain possession of the ball as it bounces off after a missed shot.

Rebound energy. The energy a ball gains when bouncing back from impact.

Receiver. The member of the offense who catches passes and runs toward the goal line.

Resistance. A force that slows down (or stops) motion.

Return. Hitting or passing the ball to an opponent.

Rib cage. The structure in your upper-body formed by your ribs and the bones they attach to.

Rugby. A highly physical team sport in which players carry, throw, or kick the ball to reach the goal and score points.

Runner. A person who runs for exercise, fun, or in races.

Screwball. A pitched ball with reverse spin that curves in the direction away from which it was thrown.

Serve. To hit a ball into play.

Sidespin. Moving the ball so that it spins horizontally.

Side stitch. A sharp pain under the ribcage during exercise. Avoid them by limiting food and drink before exercise.

Skateboard. A short board with four wheels that you can stand on to ride, or even to do stunts.

Skateboarding. Rolling on a skateboard, for fun, for transportation, or to compete in events.

Skier. An athlete traveling on skis (long, flat runners that attach to each foot and glide over snow or water).

Skydiver. A person who jumps out of an airplane and rides air currents.

Skydiving. To jump from a great height and freefall until opening a parachute for landing.

Slap shot. A big swing with a hockey stick, which strikes the puck with a fast, powerful stroke.

Slipstream. The area of reduced pressure behind an object moving quickly through a substance.

Snowboard. A piece of sports equipment used to ride down snowy slopes. It looks like a small surfboard.

Snowboarding. A sport in which the athlete rides a snowboard down snowy slopes, bound to the snowboard.

Soccer ball. A round, inflated ball used to play soccer.

Soles. The undersides of shoes.

Speed. The ratio of distance traveled by an object to the time spent traveling that distance.

Speed skater. An athlete who races around an oval track of ice on skates.

Sphere. A rounded, spherical object.

Spike. To drive a ball down quickly and at a sharp angle.

Spiral motion. To move in an increasing or decreasing curve around a center point.

Spirometer. A tool for measuring the amount and speed of inhalation and exhalation.

Spirometry. A test of lung function.

Spitball. An illegal, hard-to-hit pitch.

Sprinter. An athlete who specializes in running very fast for short distances, usually on a track.

Stationary. Not moving.

Stockcar racing. Racing cars around a track.

Stride. The distance covered in a step.

Strike. When a batter misses a pitch, or when a player knocks over all the pins and scores the highest points.

Strike out. When a batter misses three pitches, putting him out of the game.

Substance. Anything that takes up space and has mass.

Sweet spot. It is best to hit a ball with this part of a bat or racquet, where forces are completely balanced.

Swimmer. A person who moves through water using his arms and legs. Ways of swimming include the butterfly, backstroke, breaststroke, and freestyle.

Tackle. To stop a player who is carrying (in American football) or dribbling (in international football) the ball.

Teeing off. To start a game by hitting a ball off of a tee, or with a long throw.

Tennis. A game played by two players or two pairs on a court divided by a net. Players hit a ball back and forth with racquets.

Terminal velocity. The maximum velocity a falling object can attain due to gravity and air resistance.

Terrain. The topography or surface features of land.

Tetherball. A game involving striking a ball attached to the top of a pole by a cord.

Thrust. The force that causes an object to move, usually in the direction of forward or up.

Topspin. The forward spin put on a ball when it's hit.

Touchdown. Scoring points by getting the ball across the opponent's goal line.

Tour de France. A bicycle race that lasts three weeks and covers more than 3,000 miles. It's held in France.

Track cyclist. An athlete who participates in bike races on a track, often riding specially designed bikes.

Traction. Friction from being pulled across a surface.

Training. Preparing for an athletic event.

Trajectory. The path of a projectile as it moves.

Trap. To gain control of a moving soccer ball by allowing it to hit your foot or leg.

Triathlon. A race with swimming, cycling, and running portions, performed in that order, without rest.

Turbulence. The disorderly flow of a fluid.

Turbulent flow. The opposite of laminar flow.

Ultimate. A non-contact team sport using some of the rules of football and soccer, played with a flying disc.

Upward force. Any force directed up, such as from air resistance. It can counteract the force of gravity.

Variables. Factors that can change.

Vault. A gymnastic event in which an athlete springs onto a raised apparatus to perform a choreographed routine.

Velocity. The rate at which an object moves in a specified direction.

Vibrations. Rapid motion back and forth.

Volleyball. A game played by two teams who use their hands to try to hit a round, inflated ball over a net.

Vortex. A whirling mass of water or air.

Wake. A visible track of turbulence left by something moving through a fluid.

Watts. Units for measuring power. An electric watt is the amount of current multiplied by volts.

Williams, Venus. An American tennis player.

Wipeout. To fall off a surfboard, skateboard, or bicycle.

Work. The transfer of energy between objects.

Wrestling. A competition is which two opponents grip and try to pin and hold the other to the floor.

Acknowledgments

A standing ovation for my football-loving wife Michele Mercer; thanks for being my cheerleader, listening to my silly ideas, and being my best friend.

A polite golf clap for my daughter Nicole; thank you for occasionally taking a nap so I could write.

Three cheers for my sister Susie; thanks for all your help, and for letting me use ghost runners in Wiffle Ball when we were kids.

Thank you to the championship editorial team at Lark for providing guidance and an opportunity. Joe Rhatigan, Veronika Alice Gunter, Rain Newcomb, Rose McLarney, and Wolf Hoelscher are all-stars in every sense of the word. Veronika, you deserve a Most Valuable Editor trophy for all your patience, assistance, and great ideas.

Tom LaBaff, you deserve a gold medal for your fabulously fun illustrations of bike-riding kids, bouncing balls, and more. Your artwork scores every time and makes me smile.

Thank you Celia Naranjo, Robin Gregory, and Bradley Norris, for envisioning and producing every well-designed page. You served an ace.

Metrics

To convert degrees Fahrenheit to degrees Celsius, subtract 32 and then multiply by .56.

To convert inches to centimeters, multiply by 2.5.

To convert ounces to grams, multiply by 28.

To convert teaspoons to milliliters, multiply by 5.

To convert tablespoons to milliliters, multiply by 15.

To convert fluid ounces to milliliters, multiply by 30.

To convert cups to liters, multiply by .24.

Index